D0931261

PR
4714
.C6

1-60946

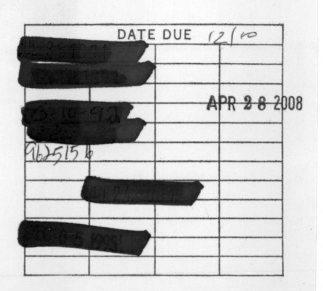

W. S. GILBERT: STAGE DIRECTOR

THE STUDENT'S MUSIC LIBRARY—HISTORICAL AND CRITICAL SERIES
Edited by PERCY M. YOUNG

W. S. GILBERT:
Stage Director

by

WILLIAM COX-IFE

London
DENNIS DOBSON

First published in Great Britain in 1977 by
Dobson Books Ltd., 80 Kensington Church Street, London, W.8
Printed by Clarke, Doble & Brendon Ltd.,
Plymouth and London

ISBN 0 234 77206 9

CONTENTS

ACKNOWLEDGEMENTS

The author would have wished to acknowledge the assistance of former colleagues in the D'Oyly Carte Opera Company—especially Martyn Green. The editor and publishers are grateful to Miss Wendy Hall for her help under difficult circumstances.

LIST OF ILLUSTRATIONS

PREFACE

William Cox-Ife (1903-68) was educated at the Royal Academy of Music, where he studied conducting under the legendary Henry J. Wood. In the early part of his career (following the early example of his master) he undertook the direction of numerous amateur choral, and operatic, societies. After the Second World War, during which he served with the Intelligence Corps, Cox-Ife extended and intensified his interests, conducting in Germany and Belgium and, at home, for films, musicals, and television.

In 1950 Cox-Ife joined the D'Oyly Carte Opera Company as Choral Director, Conductor, and Assistant Musical Director. For the remainder of his life Gilbert and Sullivan overtopped all other interests (and they were many), and Cox-Ife rendered immense service to this most English of traditions through an irresistible combination of sensitive understanding and high professional skill.

A practical man, Cox-Ife knew his subject from the working end of the theatre and his previous books testify to his ability to convey his knowledge to others. In the present instance he is characteristically informative, but also trenchant in criticism. His study of Gilbert as a revolutionary stage director (which stood as the title of this book until second thoughts took over) is timely. Not only because few persons have ever seriously considered Gilbert in this role, but also because of the zeal which producers of the "Savoy Operas" frequently show in establishing claims for their own originality. In addition to this, the fact that we know what Gilbert wanted—not only wanted but insisted on—

gives rise to wider questions in respect both of drama and music.

As Mr. Darlington says in his Foreword we do not know the final form of the conclusion of this book, for it was lost in a tragic air accident on March 24, 1968, in which Cox-Ife died. During the preparation of the text for publication the situation was made sadly more difficult through the death of the author's widow. Cox-Ife had discussed various issues concerning the ultimate shape of the book when we met for the last time. The substance of these discussions have naturally been taken into account. This applies also to the bibliography and the selection of illustrations which have been prepared by the editor.

In the years that have elapsed since Cox-Ife's death fresh impetus has been given to Gilbert and Sullivan production through the kind of consideration that is inevitably accorded to works of art after an initial posthumous period of casual indifference. This is explained by Mr. Darlington in his Foreword. Previously unfamiliar items in the canon—such as the delightful and historically important *Utopia Limited, Grand Duke* and *Princess Ida*, have been taken back into the D'Oyly Carte repertoire*, while the recent reorientation of production values in respect of the Company's *Iolanthe* make Cox-Ife's words the more significant.

P.M.Y.

1977

* Recordings of these works by the Company are, respectively: Decca SKL 5225–6, 5239–40, 4708–9.

FOREWORD

This Foreword to William Cox-Ife's book, which I had promised him to write as an act of friendship, in the end turned out to be a valediction. It was only a few weeks after our last meeting, when he finally cleared away some doubts I had had whether I was a fit and proper person to write such an introduction, when he was lost in the Irish Sea.

I was always in full agreement with his main theme: that W. S. Gilbert, as a dramatist, had always had the clearest possible idea what his characters were like and how they should be played; and that the characters of the Savoy operas, even though their author involves them in situations of fantasy, are seen as real people and must be acted as such. I was also in agreement with his view of Gilbert as a producer, and his contention that Gilbert's insistent discipline when the operas were first staged had been an important—perhaps the most important—contribution to their success.

Where I thought our opinions might diverge, and very sharply, was over the stage direction of the Gilbert and Sullivan operas for the last half-century or so. Cox-Ife was for many years a distinguished and loyal servant of the D'Oyly Carte organization. I, for many more years, have been steadily critical of that organization's policy of preserving, as if in a deep-freeze, Gilbert's methods of production. By adopting this policy, and persisting in it far too long, it did the cause of Gilbert and Sullivan a profound disservice—not in commercial terms, of course, but in terms of artistic prestige. In spite of their continued and unique popular success with their own devoted public, the Savoy operas are today held in undeserved

11

derision or contempt by a surprising number of discriminating playgoers; and if you enquire into the reason for this, it almost always turns out to be the out-of-date, almost fossilized, method of production.

The decline can be very simply illustrated. When I was an undergraduate, the visits of the D'Oyly Carte Company to Oxford and Cambridge were events of real importance. The rush for seats was phenomenal, and unless you were prepared to join the queue at about 6 a.m., your chance of getting in was small. But in those days Gilbert was still alive, still writing, still keeping a sharp eye on the operas, which had in consequence some kind of claim to be regarded as contemporary works.

Ten or fifteen years after Gilbert's death, this enthusiasm had utterly vanished. The universities were no longer interested in Gilbert and Sullivan. "In my day," said an Oxford man of about that time to me, "nobody with any claim to taste dreams of visiting the D'Oyly Carte productions. We all thought of them as museum pieces which had somehow become a cult. The idea that they were still alive, or still good, never crossed our minds. I had to find out for myself, much later, that they are the most glorious send-up of grand opera ever written."

It was inevitable that as time went on and musical plays developed in their scope, Gilbert's methods should come to seem positively primitive. Particularly was this so in his handling of the chorus, which in his day had consisted of singers whose skill as actors or dancers could not be relied on. By contrast with the modern "musical", with its chorus of highly-trained athletes who can sing, dance and (at a pinch) act, the D'Oyly Carte Company, while finding no difficulty in keeping a faithful following, fell further behind the times, with the result that today Gilbert and Sullivan are grossly undervalued by most leaders of the theatrical professions.

Feeling as I did about this, I read Cox-Ife's book with a certain trepidation, and reached the end of it without quite knowing whether I could write for him a suitable introduction. When we talked things over, however, we quickly found that we were in solid agreement on all the important points. He, no more than I, approved of the freezing effect of Gilbert's now hopelessly out-of-date style of production; it was Gilbert's sense of character that he wanted to see preserved; and because he had not made this crystal clear in the first draft of the book, he decided to add an elucidatory chapter.

This chapter he did indeed write, and told his wife that he thought that it would please both her and me when we came to read it. Unhappily, we never did read it. He had it with him in Ireland on his last trip, and it perished with him.

What that chapter contained can now never be known in detail; but an outline of what its author intended to say may be helpful to his readers. It is in that hope that I have written this account of my discussions with him.

W. A. DARLINGTON
April, 1968

13

1

EARLY DAYS

Young Gilbert, according to all accounts, was clever but lazy. But, thanks to a remarkable memory and a rooted dislike of taking second place, he would periodically get down to some hard work in order to carry off a coveted prize.

He was born at 17, Southampton Street, Strand, on November 18, 1836, one of four children. His father, William Gilbert (1804-90), was an ex-Naval Surgeon; his mother, Anne Morris, a Scot. The name Schwenk was that of his German godmother. Thanks to a legacy which left him moderately well-off, William Gilbert had left the Navy early in his career and was able to spend much of his time travelling in Europe, chiefly Germany and Italy, with his wife and young son. In fact it was when the family were in Naples with William Schwenk, then aged two, that an incident occurred that was reflected some forty-odd years later in *The Pirates of Penzance*. The child was left in the charge of "a simple nursery maid", who, when two respectable-looking men approached and told her that they had been asked to take the boy back to his parents, handed him over without further ado. He was then held for ransom for the magnificent sum of £25 which was hastily paid and the boy returned unharmed.

This incident did not, however, deter his parents from sending him at the age of seven, to a school in Boulogne where he stayed for nearly six years. He then returned to England and continued his education at Great Ealing School, London. This was a grammar school famous for the scholastic achievements of the pupils amongst whom were to be found many famous names, including those of William Makepeace

Thackeray, Bishop Selwyn, Thomas Huxley and his brothers and Walter Besant. Within three years Gilbert was head of his school and distinguished as a translator of Greek and Latin verses. It was not evident, at the time, whence he derived his obvious literary talent, but later, much later, it became clear that it was from his father.

Gilbert senior, seeing his son becoming, in his late twenties, a writer of some repute, decided that what the son could do, so could the father. (Like his son he did not care to take second place!) Although his writings were successful in their day, his three volume novels, portentous dissertations, and biographies written in the stilted literary style of the period, are not acceptable to modern readers; especially as he was always stressing his aversion to some aspect of everyday life, thereby filling many of his works with fulminations against intemperance, and injustices to ratepayers, and making no secret of his dislike of the Roman Church. All this despite the fact that he had a strong sense of the ridiculous which was inherited by his son.

It cannot be denied, however, that he had a rightful claim to be considered a man of wide interests and catholic tastes. Here are the titles of some of his works which reflect the vigorous intellect that was undoubtedly also to be found in Gilbert junior.

Facta non Verba. A comparison between the good works performed by the ladies in Roman Catholic Convents in England and the unfettered efforts of their Protestant Sisters (1874).

Shirley Hall Asylum or The Memoirs of a Monomaniac (1863).

The Magic Mirror. A round of tales for young and old, with 84 illustrations by W. S. G. (1865).

Lucrezia Borgia. A biography. Illustrated by rare and unpublished documents (1869).

King George's Middy. Illustrated by W. S. G. (1869).

Nothing but the Truth. An unvarnished picture of the effects of intemperance (1877).

Modern Wonders of the World or The New Sinbad (1881).

George Grossmith, 1888

Richard D'Oyly Carte, 1891

"Spy" cartoons in *Vanity Fair.*

Sir Arthur Sullivan, 1874

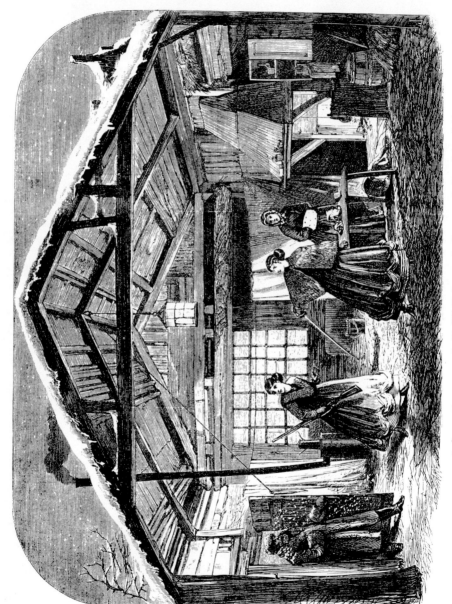

A dramatic moment in T. W. Robertson's *Ours*, 20th October, 1866.

Even as a child William Schwenk Gilbert showed a marked disposition to domineer and this undoubtedly did much to make him unpopular with his fellow students, although it certainly helped him make a success of almost everything that he attempted. He was an inveterate reader and handy with pen and pencil as many of his contemporaries, at a later date, learnt to their discomfiture.

As the boy grew into the man, other traits of character became evident. He was incurably straightforward and out-spoken and had an irritating passion for accuracy. He was kindly but quick tempered and liable to take offence easily. His apparent straight-laced attitude towards life was surely rooted in his "deep and sincere regard for religion and good men and women of all faiths."[1] Vulgarity of any kind was abhorrent to him.

As a boy Gilbert had a passion for the stage and actors and it was whilst he was still at school that the first glimpse of the future man of the theatre could have been observed. For it was then that he wrote his first plays, painted their scenery and, of course, acted as stage-manager, albeit a very forceful one who, it is said, was prepared to back his instructions with physical force!

It is a pity that there are no records of these first efforts for it was not a family habit to keep any correspondence and papers, once they had served their purpose. Fortunately for us today, Gilbert conquered this indifference to the written record when he was a young man, as the Gilbert archives in the British Museum and elsewhere show.

On leaving Great Ealing School he went to King's College, London, one of the colleges of the University of London, where, at the age of nineteen, he took his Bachelor of Arts degree. He then read for an examination in order to get a commission in the Army with the idea of taking part in the Crimean war. Fortunately peace was declared before he had

[1] Sidney Dark & Rowland Grey, *William Schwenk Gilbert, his life and letters*, Methuen & Co., 1923, p. 2.

completed the course and he turned to the Civil Service, obtaining an assistant-clerkship in the Education Department of the Privy Council—"in which ill-organized and ill-governed office I spent four uncomfortable years,"[1] he afterwards wrote. One can presume that they were also uncomfortable years for his colleagues, as it is hard to imagine the satirical tongue being still for so long a period!

He next tried his hand at the Law and entered the Inner Temple, finally, in 1866 joining the Northern Circuit as a fully-fledged barrister. He also attended the Old Bailey and other courts and spent four fruitless years of practice averaging about five cases per year. It is said that he was such a poor advocate that his first client, a woman, on losing her case, stood up in the dock, removed her shoe and threw it at him! Also, whilst attending the Inner Temple he had secured a commission as ensign in the 5th West Yorks Militia. The Militia was somewhat similar to our Territorial Army and as a "part-time" officer he transferred, in 1865, to the Royal Aberdeenshire Militia with which he stayed until 1878. It was whilst in this regiment that he had the privilege of wearing the kilt.[2]

But if these years as a barrister were fruitless from the point of view of pecuniary reward, they were manifestly fruitful in that he was able to find ample time for writing whilst waiting for the briefs which came only but rarely. It was surely these years of frustration in the Civil Service and the legal world that helped sharpen the edge of his satire.

When he was twenty-four a newspaper called *Fun* was published, and at last Gilbert had a humorous article together with a drawing accepted. This started the ball rolling and for ten years he was a regular contributor to this rival of *Punch* and also acted as their dramatic critic. So, with no deliberate intent upon his part, Gilbert became connected with the

[1] From an article by Gilbert in *Theatre*.
[2] E. G. M. Bullock, "Gilbert's Soldiering Days," *G. & S. Journal*, Vol. I, No. 2.

theatre, and at the same time he produced the first examples of his divine sense of the ridiculous in *The Bab Ballads* which were to offer him many a source of inspiration when the Savoy Operas came into being. Edith Browne who wrote the first study of Gilbert in 1907 says: "Moreover he is not a *funny* man; he is a very serious man and therein lies the irresistible charm of that peculiar quality known as Gilbertian humour. The term 'Gilbertian' is descriptive of a conflict between the well-balanced mind of a serious man and the exuberant spirit of his impish counterpart; the imp triumphs, but according to the terms of the treaty between the two, the serious mortal is allowed to keep his intelligence and to make believe that he does not see anything funny in the little imp's delightful nonsense. By this compact all intelligent mortals are saved the pain of watching their fellow men obviously playing the buffoon."[1]

But, important as was his development as a writer during this period of his life, he would not have taken his rightful place in the history of the English theatre had it not been for his friendship with Tom Robertson, playwright and stage-manager.[2] This came about when Gilbert formed a small club of his fellow writers on *Fun*, called "Serious Family", and it was at the regular Saturday night meetings at his chambers in Grays Inn that Gilbert's acquaintanceship with Robertson ripened into a lasting friendship. Most important of all was Robertson's invitation to Gilbert to attend, whenever possible, any rehearsals that he, Robertson, was holding. It so happened that Robertson was the founder of an entirely new style of stage technique and management.[3] To use Gilbert's own words, Robertson "invented stage management". Even so this knowledge that Gilbert absorbed by attendance at these rehearsals would have been wasted had he not during this period become a successful playwright, but the English stage owes a debt to Robertson for teaching Gilbert to be his own

[1] Edith A. Browne, *W. S. Gilbert*, John Lane, 1907, p. 3.
[2] See p. 23   [3] See p. 25

19

stage-manager and for getting him his first commission to write a burlesque for the Christmas season at the St. James's Theatre.

So, at the age of thirty, this young man stood at the threshold of a career as dramatist and director which was going to bring a delight to the English-speaking theatre that, after nine decades of non-stop performances, has still to be equalled.

2

REFORMS IN PRODUCTION

According to G. M. Trevelyan the nineteenth century "was an age of transition from aristocracy to democracy, from authority to mass-judgment".[1] This period of transition saw the beginnings of great changes in the way of life for "the people", and there were changes in literature and thought, as well as in society and politics. Unfortunately this period of change had little, if any, influence on the theatre. It is a depressing experience to read the lists of theatrical productions of this century in Allardyce Nicoll's books upon the drama, and even more depressing to read some of the plays themselves. For, in spite of the work of the truly great legitimate actors of the day during the greater part of the century, the theatre remained at very low ebb; "melodrama, burlesque, sentimental comedy and low buffoonery ruled without a rival."[2] The "typical audiences [in the first half of the century] were composed mainly of lower-class citizens with a sprinkling of representatives from the gayer and more libertine section of the aristocracy. The staid middle class and the respectable, dignified nobility tended to look upon the stage as a thing not to be supported in an active manner."[3]

John Hollingshead, the famous theatre manager who for many years ran the old Gaiety Theatre, described himself as "a licensed dealer in legs, short skirts, French adaptations, Shakespeare, taste and musical glasses!" Small wonder that

[1] G. M. Trevelyan, English Social History, Longmans, 1944, p. 522.
[2] Allardyce Nicoll, A History of English Drama, Cambridge University Press, 1959, V, p. 109.
[3] ibid., pp. 8–9.

Henry Morley, the newly appointed Professor of English Literature in University College, London, wrote: "There will be no want of good plays when they have room to come up, and are not choked by the bad burlesques and French translations that now occupy the ground."[1] And further: ". . . burlesque, vacuity of thought giving itself all the airs of wit, and most dependent for success on a display of women's legs and servile copies of the humour of the music-halls".[2]

Dickens, in his job as dramatic critic, wrote of the audience (in his notice of Macready in the role of Benedick) ". . . nobility and gentry . . . who, when they repair to an English temple of drama, would seem to be attracted hither solely by an amiable desire to purify by their presence a scene of vice and indecorum". Strong words, perhaps even a trifle exaggerated, but not without cause. John Hare, the actor, found things in 1856 in "a parlous state . . . most of the plays that were not classics revived, were poor, and the playgoers proved singularly apathetic." And, as an example of the writing typical of the so-called comedies of the period the following from *The First Night*, by J. M. Maddox, produced at the Princess's Theatre, London, in 1853, speaks for itself.

> C'est egal—I am her fader—the public shall excuse me—attendez—Allons ma fille! Mais stop—what I see? dere is a public here also! Oh! dear me! mais courage! perhaps dey will be so kind as de oder public dere. I shall presume to take the liberty to ask dem!
> Messeurs and Mesdames.
>
>> We've had applause behind the scene,
>> I've tickled dem 'tis true,
>> But dat, alas is leetel worth
>> Unless I tickle you.
>> Ah say, den dat de debutante
>> Again shall reappear,

[1] Henry Morley, *The Journal of a London Playgoer from 1851 to 1866*, George Routledge & Sons, 1866, p. 10.
[2] ibid., p. 25

And let de plaudits over dere
Now find an echo here.

It is therefore not surprising that such fare was looked upon with disapproval by the Victorian middle-class paterfamilias whose stern sense of respectability deterred him from exposing his wife and family to such unworthy spectacles.

Gilbert also had his say: "When my collaboration with Sir Arthur Sullivan began, English comic opera had practically ceased to exist and such musical entertainments as held the stage were adaptations of operas by Offenbach, Audran, Lecocq. Their treatment was crude, unintelligent and sometimes frankly improper."

Obviously the time for reform in the theatre was ripe and the first move in this direction was made by Tom Robertson whose work marked the beginning of the revolution, not only in writing for the theatre, but in stage direction as well. He was a true man of the theatre having been, at various times of his life, author, actor, manager, prompter, scene-painter and even stage carpenter, and it was in 1865 that he opened the door upon an entirely fresh field of writing and stage management. His work for the theatre in these two fields also brought to light the fact, hitherto unthought of, that style of writing and style of direction are inseparable and must be complementary one to the other. Prior to this time, owing to the moribund state of play-writing, dialogue and character names might differ, but the so-called interpretation of the roles remained the same and instead of true characterization all that was offered comprised a few conventional mannerisms guaranteed to have effect upon an unenlightened audience. This deplorable standard of performance was further aggravated by the star system in which the star was of paramount importance, and provided the play gave opportunities for scenes in which he or she dominated all was well. Little else received much attention and the rest of the cast were left to their own devices as long as they did not interfere with the star. In fact woe betide any supporting actor who had the temerity to attract the critics by the quality of his acting! The function of the stage-manager was merely to conduct rehearsals and keep discipline. He "ranked as only a kind of superior foreman and had no say in the aesthetic conception or interpretation of the play."[1]

Tom Robertson's play *Society* was the first real attempt by a playwright to offer the audience realism in place of artificiality. And such a revolution in the writing called for a similar revolution in production. In fact the one could not have come into being without the other. At last reality came to the theatre, in the characters of the play and in their speech, behaviour, and in their surroundings. Small as the detail may seem to modern eyes, the "practical" door, seen for the first time on the stage, was indicative of the new approach.

Two years later in 1867 Robertson wrote and produced *Caste*, the most significant play of this period. His new approach to production came as a great shock to the audience of the day.

> . . . Love scenes unlike anything that an audience had at that date seen. The dialogue presents a natural development of conversation between two lovers; their meeting is brusque, unemotional, almost cool, yet the scene contrives to suggest impassioned feeling more subtly than could be done with the aid of fiery speeches in the Claude Melnotte style. It was a deliberate part of Robertson's technique to divest love scenes of all extravagant elements, stressing constantly the importance of small detail, endowing it with that significance which it assumes in actual life. . . . This realistic treatment proved a startling reform to audiences more accustomed to long speeches couched in terms of the age of chivalry than to natural conversation. . . . The deliberate artlessness of the love scenes was at first mistaken for pusillanimity and their realism confused with

[1] Richard Findlater, *The Unholy Trade*, Gollancz, 1952, p. 94.

a want of dramatic technique. Actually Robertson's technique was of a very high order.[1]

Sir John Hare, the famous actor, said,

My opinion of Robertson as a stage manager is of the very highest order. He had a peculiar gift to himself, and which I have never seen in any other author, of conveying by some rapid and almost electrical suggestion to the actor an insight into the character assigned to him. As nature was the basis of his own work, so he sought to make actors understand it should be theirs. He thus founded a school of natural acting which completely revolutionized the then existing methods, and by so doing did incalculable good to the stage.[2]

Gilbert himself said that "Robertson invented stage management", and it was by being present at so many of Robertson's rehearsals that he, Gilbert, learnt the fundamentals of production as well as playwriting. He was quick to grasp the importance of this new approach to writing and production, and in spite of the topsy-turvy world of make-believe in which so many of his works are set it is the realism of his dialogue and settings, and the behaviour of his characters that point the edge of the satire.

His first work for the stage was *Dulcamara*, commissioned at Robertson's suggestion by the lessee of the St. James's Theatre for the Christmas season of 1866. This was a burlesque on *L'Elisir d'Amore*, and it afforded no breakaway from the popular burlesques of the period. This was followed by 22 stage productions from burlesque and extravaganza to drama and comedy. A superabundance of experiment in the successful production of theatrical plays, and, although these works marked a great improvement upon those of his predecessors, he had not yet developed the vein of satire that became the foundation of his comic operas; neither was the general style of these works in any way revolutionary. They could not be

[1] Ernest Reynolds, *Early Victorian Drama*, Heffer & Son, 1936, p. 86.
[2] T. W. Robertson, *Society* and *Caste* (ed. T. E. Pemberton), D. C. Heath & Co., 1905, p. xxxi.

25

said "to prepare directly for the operas or reveal the characteristics of their humour." [1]

It is a simple matter to trace Gilbert's development as a playwright for there are the plays themselves to be studied, but it is not so straightforward when thinking of Gilbert the producer. Here the evidence has to be culled from letters and press notices and the latter are not always as informative as one would wish for. This new "invention production" was not yet deemed sufficiently significant in the minds of contemporary critics to be worthy of detailed comment.

Bearing in mind that the accepted method of production of the day was, "Give the actors the script and let them sort it out," and also the fact that Gilbert was still feeling his way as a producer, he was fortunate in having in the cast of his better plays of this period such established performers as the Kendals (W. H. and his wife Madge Robertson, Tom Robertson's sister), Forbes Robertson and Marion Terry. One can be sure that whilst still adhering to the "star" system of presentation, they "sorted things out" to good effect. Nevertheless this did not satisfy Gilbert who maintained a running battle against the "star" performer to whose egoism he refused to submit, in spite of the financial rewards that were coming his way—rewards that were to a considerable degree due to the popularity of the stars themselves. Gilbert was, however, unshakable in his determination to have his way and it is not surprising to read the following letter from W. H. Kendal —the"star" was turning!

1874

Dear Gilbert,

Will you come here tomorrow morning and read the piece [*Sweethearts*] over to us—say at 11 o'clock? If you are off on Saturday it will be our only chance of getting your invaluable suggestions. I think we shall learn more from your reading the piece to us and explaining the situations etc. as you go along,

[1] Ashley H. Thorndike, *English Comedy*, Macmillan, N.Y., 1929, p. 450.

than struggling through it for the first time on the stage—what think you? Have you sketches of costumes—they will be of great assistance to us if you have?

With mutual kind regards,
W. H. K.

Again in November 1876 the famous American actor Sothern wrote,

give me every possible suggestion as to the business of each character. I will carry out your ideas to the best of my ability— be sure and send me most complete sketches and ground plots. O'Connor, the scenic artist of the Theatre Royal, Haymarket, or Oliver Wells, the master carpenter, can make lovely working models and I will pay for them.

Then in December,

Let me have full scene and property plots—colours of curtains etc., etc. I want the play to be beautifully produced.

The true stage-director was emerging, proving to be a very different person from the accepted stage-manager of earlier decades. Gilbert was justifying his authoritarian attitude and it was in the style in which comedy should be played that he was adamant. When his comedy *Engaged* was about to be produced he gave instructions to the company that can be regarded as the yardstick for all time in playing comedy and farce. Here they are—

It is absolutely essential to the success of this piece that it should be played with the most perfect earnestness and gravity throughout. There should be no exaggeration in costume, make-up, or demeanour; and the characters, one and all, should appear to believe, throughout, in the perfect sincerity of their words and actions. Directly the actors show that they are conscious of the absurdity of their utterances the piece begins to drag.

To treat a thoroughly farcical subject in a thoroughly serious manner became Gilbert's formula and herein lay the strength of his work as playwright and director; writing and directing being so interlinked that his characters, as set down in the book, were no vague creations waiting for life to be given them by the actor, but ones which the author had visualized down to the last detail. This was Gilbert's first step in direction—the delineation of character. There is, moreover, documentary proof of Gilbert's care in this respect with reference to his play *Dan'l Druce*, written in 1875, for which he gives the following detailed description of each character.

> *Sir Jasper Graeme* (1st Act): a rollicking dare-devil, dissipated cavalier—age 40. (2nd and 3rd Acts) A grave, sober country gentleman, age 54.
>
> *Abel Druce* (1st Act): A hard crossed-grained miserly misanthrope—living alone in a hut by the sea-shore. (2nd and 3rd Acts) The same, reformed, a tender-hearted genial old man—passionately fond of his supposed daughter and broken-hearted when there's a chance of losing her—Strong character part—pathos and passion.
>
> *Reuben Haines:* Quaint, high dried humorous scoundrel.
>
> *May:* A simple Puritan girl—Quakerish in manner of speaking and demure.
>
> *Dorothy:* her friend—a contrast—a village girl with rather worldly views—coquettish and pretty.
>
> *Geoffrey Wyngard:* A good-looking young merchant-mate in love with May—boyish and impulsive.

Such care for detail was far removed from the slipshod standards of production when roles were simply assigned to the actors with no discussion of the relation of a part to the total play and when, furthermore, stereotyped characterization was accepted. In this detailed cast list can been seen the influence of his mentor Robertson who, only a few years earlier in 1871, had prefaced his play *War* with the following injunctions:

> The author requests this part [Col de Rochevanne] may be played with a slight French accent. He is not to pronounce his words *absurdly* or shrug his shoulders, or duck his head towards his stomach, like conventional stage Frenchmen. Col de Roche-

vanne is to be played with the old pre-Revolutionary politeness
—knightly courtesy, with a mixture of ceremony and bonhomie.

This part [Herr Karl Hartmann] to be played with a slight
German accent and not to be made wilfully comic. Herr Karl
Hartmann is to be played a perfect gentleman, with a touch of
the pedant in his manner—but always a gentleman.

Captain Sound is not to be dressed in uniform, but in the
morning dress of a gentleman. His manner is to be hearty but
not rough; in every aspect that of a captain of a man-of-war,
and not the master of a half-penny steamboat.

Being his own director and therefore not finding it
necessary to commit to paper his ideas in full, we do not find
in the prompt-books of the Gilbert and Sullivan Operas
detailed delineation of character, but in the libretti unmistakable pointers to character are to be found. For example
what clearer indication of Shadbolt's temperament could be
given than that found in his remarks to Phoebe in the opening scene of *The Yeomen of the Guard*?

These allusions to my professional duties are in doubtful taste.
I didn't become a head-jailer because I like head-jailing. I
didn't become an assistant-tormentor because I like assistant-
tormenting.

And a little later in the same scene:

I'm jealous of everybody and everything. I'm jealous of the
very words I speak to you because they reach your ears—and I
mustn't go near 'em!

Having a clear conception of a character in one's mind and
persuading an actor to give a true portrayal of that conception
are two different things. But this is precisely what Gilbert, as
a general rule, was able to do. His methods of achieving this
were not always palatable to some of his cast for he was an
autocrat of the first water and made no effort to disguise the
fact. He once said of the productions of the Savoy Operas,
"my distinguished co-worker [Sullivan] and myself exercised
the most absolute and undisputed control over the productions of our pieces", and he could have added "thanks to the

vision of Richard D'Oyly Carte who gave us his never-ceasing support in this respect". William Archer, the great theatre critic, said that Gilbert's was

> The most striking individuality, the most original character our theatre of today can boast. . . . The very fact that he is personally by no means popular in the theatrical world is not without its significance. This may arise partly from adventitious circumstances, such as his severity as a stage-manager—a severity which produces admirable results—and may be partly due to absolute faults of character . . . in such a world as that of the London theatres no one can be thoroughly popular who is not either an accomplished Philistine or an accomplished hypocrite.[1]

And of Gilbert the playwright he had written, "How many of our English authors possess enough force of character and mastery of the stage to impose their conceptions upon the autocratic actor-manager? One perhaps—W. S. Gilbert."

There is, amongst his letters, record of one occasion upon which an actor deliberately ignored Gilbert's instructions as to how an important scene should be played. This occurred in 1878 when Gilbert produced his play *The Ne'er do Weel*. In a letter written some years later to Mr Eli Wallach he said—

> It failed, owing as I believe, to the egregious buffoonery of the actor who played "Quilt". I had previously cautioned him, at rehearsal, that if the scene at the end of Act 2 was not played quietly and with perfect seriousness, the situation would utterly fail. He insisted on "clowning" through the scene and the audience hooted at him. The third act began with a long scene between him and the actor who played the sea-captain O. *The audience would not listen to one word of this*—they howled through the entire scene and its purport was utterly lost.

But autocrat that he was he knew when to advise and when to leave the actors alone. In 1888 a special performance

[1] William Archer, *English Dramatists of To-day*, Sampson, Low, Marston, Searle & Rivington, 1882, p. 148.

of *Pygmalion and Galatea* was given by a distinguished cast headed by Miss Mary Anderson. In the cast was a newcomer to the stage, Miss Julia Neilson, a discovery of Gilbert's. Of the rehearsals he said,

> . . . with the exception of Miss Neilson (whom, as a novice, I instructed in the elocutionary treatment of her speeches, but whose gestures and actions I left absolutely uncontrolled) I rarely interfered with the people concerned except when appealed to by them.

It can be assumed that his direction of the novice was successful for, as the one notice of this performance which I could find, says:

> Miss Julia Neilson has made a first appearance of great promise, in the character of Cynisca, from Mr Gilbert's *Pygmalion and Galatea*. She is tall, graceful, with a fine stage face and a musical voice and so clever a newcomer will be very welcome.

In the next few months Gilbert gave Julia Neilson a few isolated performances in the lesser roles in other plays of his, and then cast her for a leading part in the first production of his play *Brantingham Hall*. This time he was not so successful. The *Daily Telegraph* said:

> [Miss Neilson's performance] was very measured, deliberate, and often painfully slow—occasioned perhaps by over-tuition, possibly by nervousness. As yet the lady's view of the character wants spontaneity, sincerity and nature. We never felt that Ruth really meant what she said. . . . The same idea of over-instruction that necessarily results in the most approved form of over-acting was noticeable in the clever scenes played by Mr Duncan Fleet and Miss Rose Norreys.

There was however, in the cast, a young actor of considerable stage experience, Lewis Waller and he was able to do justice to Gilbert's direction for "as Ralph Crampton stood before us we did more than hear the words he spoke. We saw the workings of his mind" (the *Daily Telegraph*). This surely is how all good actors respond to expert direction—whether the director puts it in so many words or not, they are given an insight into the mind of the character they are portraying. As early as 1873 Gilbert had thought on these lines, for in the first rough draft of *The Wicked World* he included these directions as to how lines were to be delivered.

> The arguments used by Selene are urged with the most perfect modesty, though with a certain demure slyness and semi-consciousness that her arguments are to a certain extent specious and artificial.

As Selene was played by Madge Kendal (Mrs Robertson) we can rest assured that these instructions were carried out.

The theatrical correspondent of *The Tribune* (New York), George W. Smalley, wrote the following after his visit to London at the end of the nineteenth century.

> His [Gilbert's] panegyrists lay stress on the kindliness of his satires in his plays and operas. That is true enough, and it is also true that he was full of kindliness in his relations with his own world. But it is true also that he had an arbitrary temper. He liked to domineer. He liked his own way better than yours or mine. . . . He was a tyrant at rehearsals, and I will only add that it would be better for the English stage if more English authors had a knowledge and authority equal to his. . . . His convictions of stage discipline, and even the maxims of war on which some of them seemed to be founded, were applied with equal rigour to the training of actresses in which he perceived the seeds of art. One of them was Miss Lily Hamburg who had natural gifts which in Gilbert's hands became artificial. The other was no less a person than Miss Julia Neilson. I met now and then both Miss Julia Neilson and Gilbert and from Miss Neilson and Miss Hamburg I heard interesting accounts of the tuition he bestowed on each. He was not content to rely on nature or natural aptitudes. He had Procrustean rules on stage training to which all natural gifts must be made to bend. So many steps to a particular spot; such a gesture to express such an emotion; the arms to be moved in accord with a settled

Scene from *The Fairy's Dilemma*.

Trial by Jury, with Henry Lytton as the Judge.

The Mikado, film directed by Victor Schertzinger, 1939.

The Mikado in the D'Oyly Carte Opera Company 1964 production for
B.H.E. Productions Ltd.

theory of plastic effect, the tones of the voice to be such as the master thought most likely to come over the footlights; and so on. If in Miss Julia Neilson's mature methods there be a suspicion of anything rigid or arbitrary, it may be traced to these iron-bound laws laid down for and enforced upon her by Gilbert in the days of her girlhood.

In his dealing with the formed artists Gilbert was not less absolute. For the first night or the three hundredth night his will was law.[1]

Such rigid discipline seems, in some schools of acting, absolutely unacceptable today, but with the advent of Robertson and Gilbert and the new school of production, it was accepted in the nineteenth century. If we look across the Channel we find that such a method was not peculiar to Gilbert, especially when it was a matter of how the lines should be spoken. France had already its National Theatre, an institution as yet unknown in England, and George Smalley later in his book observed:[2]

> Yet I had often heard Sarah [Bernhardt] describe and extol the sternness of the discipline on the stage of the Français. There the *régisseur* is the master. He is more than master. He is a despot.
>
> "He has made me recite a simple line fifty times till I delivered it to please him; me, Sarah!"
>
> But in the rehearsal of a new piece the author steps in. He is then the despot, and from his decree there is no appeal.

We are surely correct in assuming that this discipline was as strict when it came to the "business" in a play. It also sheds some light upon an incident that was told me many years ago of a meeting between Sarah Bernhardt and Mrs Patrick Campbell. Bernhardt had seen Mrs Campbell in a play and gone round afterwards to congratulate her [Mrs Campbell] upon her performance. Bernhardt remarked upon one

[1] George W. Smalley, *Anglo-American Memories*, Duckworth, 1911, Ch. XXV.
[2] Vol. 2, p. 322.

C
33

particularly moving episode and suggested that it must have taken Mrs Campbell a long time to perfect. "Oh no," replied Mrs Campbell, "I just did it on the spur of the moment." "Really," commented Bernhardt, "I'm sorry, I thought you were a professional, but I see that you are just an amateur."

Such discipline as to the way in which lines are to be spoken should not, even today, be dismissed as old fashioned. Only a few weeks ago I heard a famous writer and film director, Joseph L. Mankiewicz, talking about his methods as a director and he said that when he had written the script, as he invariably does, he was adamant as to how the lines should be spoken. For as he wrote the lines, he heard in his own mind the inflections that would bring out the precise meaning. He said that he would not tolerate the "let me say it *my* way old man" approach of some actors.[1] This seems to me a reasonable stand for any author-director to take for only he can say exactly what he had in mind as he wrote.

That delightful actor, Percy Marmont, talked to me of his being directed by Gilbert in a revival of *The Palace of Truth*. "Of course," he said, "Gilbert insisted that the lines be spoken exactly as he wanted, but, at the same time, we learned to think as we spoke." In the same production another young actor who became in later years a famous director, Milton Rosmer, said in a letter to me, "he had an unerring faculty for showing you how to say a line—not always obviously funny in itself and often with a pun—with such subtly humorous inflections as to make it sound the height of wit." This was true comedy direction.

After only a decade of work in the theatre and before he had really got into his stride as a director, the following news comment speaks for itself.

Playwrights themselves, it appears, have grown weary of the eccentric and meretricious pretensions out of which they have for so long a period been constructing what was considered

[1] *Cinema with Michael Scott*, Granada Television, March 1967.

34

popular drama for mixed audiences: or education has already begun to do its work and audiences, whether mixed or select, have detected the fraudulent nature of the compound with which such strenuous endeavours have been made to satisfy the appetite of the million . . . Mr W. S. Gilbert—to his honour be it said—broke, some seasons ago, through the prevailing fashion, and attempted a quasi-poetic production, something between a masque and a burlesque, which fortunately found favour with his patrons. We have reason to congratulate him on his productions *Pygmalion and Galatea*, *The Palace of Truth*, and *The Wicked World*, which in style were certainly in advance of his time.[1]

And still there was to come what was probably Gilbert's most important contribution, both as writer and director, to the theatre, the Savoy Operas for as yet he had only one successful musical entertainment to his credit, *Trial by Jury*.

[1] *Sporting and Dramatic News*, December, 1875.

3

THE SAVOY OPERAS

Looking back upon the fortuitous circumstances that brought Gilbert and Sullivan together, it seems inevitable that these two men would meet and work in partnership. Prior to their first collaboration in 1871 they were both involved with the theatre and, each with other partners, had produced works of various types. Gilbert, in addition to his many plays and extravaganzas, a one act opera *Ages Ago* with music by a friend of Sullivan, Frederick Clay; Sullivan, the incidental music to *The Tempest, Cox and Box* to a libretto by Frank Burnand, and also *The Contrabandista* with the same librettist. In the programme which contained *Cox and Box*, Gilbert also had an "Entirely New Entertainment," *No Cards*, so although not yet partners the names of Gilbert and Sullivan were on the same playbill.

It was John Hollingshead, the "licensed dealer in legs, etc.", who brought the two men together as collaborators, and so was founded the immortal partnership. This was in the "Entirely Original Grotesque Opera", *Thespis*. Of this work only the libretto remains, the music with the exception of one song, "Little Maid of Arcadee", and a chorus used later in *The Pirates of Penzance*, is lost. The reception on the opening night was mixed—the critics praised the material, ". . . the story so original, the music so pretty and fascinating—a story so pointed and happy, the music so satisfactory and refined, a spectacle so beautiful and artists so clever", but the production was sadly under-rehearsed. Gilbert admitted that "it was put together in less than three weeks and was produced at the

Gaiety after a week's rehearsal!"[1] One can therefore assume that he had had insufficient time in which to convince his cast, principals and chorus, that the prevalent standard of production of operetta was no longer acceptable. So after sixty-four performances *Thespis* closed, never to be heard again.

But, hurried as this whole production was, one thing was evident to the discerning critics and that was the unmistakable accord between author and composer. One critic said,

> Mr Gilbert in *Thespis* has happily provided the composer with everything he could desire, mastering the character of opera-extravaganza, which precludes the exercise of the highest flights of genius of which a musician is capable, and sets a limit to the exercise of his talents.

Another said,

> Tuneful throughout, always pretty, frequently suggestive, the songs and dances are quite in character with the author's design.

In spite of the shortcomings of the presentation *Thespis* marked a major step forward in the development of light musical entertainment; the results were still evident in the theatre fifty years later.

Nevertheless, it was three years before the two got together again. During this period Gilbert had written some twelve plays and Sullivan a *Festival Te Deum*, an oratorio, *The Light of The World,* and a miscellany of popular ballads and church music. His only commission for the stage was the incidental music to *The Merry Wives of Windsor.*

In January of 1875, the shrewd young impresario Richard D'Oyly Carte brought the two together once more and this meeting proved to be a red-letter day not only for the three concerned, but for the English theatre. The outcome of this meeting, as all the world knows, was seen on the evening of March 25, 1875, when the stage was graced by the first "real" Gilbert and Sullivan collaboration, *Trial by Jury.*

[1] *Theatre,* April 1883.

It would be out of place here to extol the virtue and quality of this gem of a one act opera and indeed unnecessary, for it has already been done by other writers. The notices were enthusiastic to a degree and, once again, much was made of the rapport between the two partners. One said, ". . . so completely is each imbued with the same spirit that it would be difficult to conceive the existence of Mr Gilbert's verses without Mr Sullivan's music, as of Mr Sullivan's music without Mr Gilbert's verses." Another concurred, "It seems as though poems and music had proceeded from one and the same brain."

As yet detailed criticism of the "direction" of any play was unknown—or, at least, extremely rare—and it was generally referred to by generalities. This was so for *Trial by Jury* but we find Mr Fred Sullivan as the learned and impressionable Judge deserves a special word of praise for his "quiet and natural humour", and "the greatest 'hit' was made by Mr Fred Sullivan, whose blending of official dignity, condescension, and, at the right moment, extravagant humour, made the character of the Judge stand out with all requisite prominence". Obviously the hand of Gilbert the Director was at work with his insistence on how comedy should be played, and—to quote further—the statement that "Laughter more frequent or more hearty was never heard in any theatre than that which more than once brought the action of the 'dramatic cantata' to a temporary standstill" was additional proof of his skill in this field of work. For, in spite of the excellence of the libretto and charm of the music, mishandling on the part of a performer would have blurred the humour and blunted the satire.

Thus was the foundation stone of the Gilbert and Sullivan operas well and truly laid.

After this fantastic success, Richard D'Oyly Carte lost no time in forming his Comedy Opera Company and entering into a contract with Gilbert and Sullivan for a new operetta. This was *The Sorcerer* and in this work of two acts only is

38

to be found the pattern upon which the remaining Savoy Operas were moulded, with the exception of *Princess Ida* which was divided into Prologue and two acts. This was later altered to three acts.

By 1876 Gilbert had learnt much about the art of directing, not only from watching Tom Robertson at work, but by observing fine actors at work in his own rehearsals. Some might say that he also had a natural advantage which stood him in good stead when dealing with the casts of the Gilbert and Sullivan operas for, according to François Cellier, who was so closely associated with him for over thirty years as musical director of the D'Oyly Carte Opera Company, "he had a deep-rooted creed that actors are made, not born and that acting, being mimetic, was as much a matter of instruction as elementary mathematics".

It was when he began to produce the Gilbert and Sullivan operas that Gilbert faced, for the first time, the bugbear of the director—casting. For—to quote Cellier once more—

> It was obvious that the lesson Gilbert and Sullivan had come to teach would not precisely suit the existing school of actors and singers. There would be too much to unlearn, too much new-fangled form of study to be graciously accepted by the proud and jealous supporters of ancient histrionic traditions. The Gilbertian methods appeared at once to be only adaptable to novices in the school of acting. . . . That they (the existing performers) were clever and accomplished actors and singers of their kind, none will deny, but they had become too saturated with the obsolescent spirit of Victorian burlesque and extravaganza ever to become capable exponents of a Gilbert and Sullivan opera.[1]

In 1876, a year before *The Sorcerer* was produced, there was a case of miscasting in a Gilbert operetta, which confirmed these remarks of Cellier. Gilbert, in collaboration with Frederick Clay, had written an operetta, *Princess Toto*, for

[1] F. A. Cellier & C. Bridgeman, *Gilbert, Sullivan and D'Oyly Carte*, Pitman, London, 1914, p. 34.

Miss Kate Santley, a well-known "star" of the musical stage. In spite of the announcement in the programme, Gilbert did not produce this work. Clay did so, without consulting Gilbert on any point whatsoever. The result could hardly be called a success, as is shown by a notice of October 3, 1876:

> Unfortunately for the piece, the one performer who is out of harmony with the character she enacts, is the actress who plays Princess Toto. Miss Kate Santley is about the last of the beautiful, but barbarous tribe to whom, though devoid of all proper art-culture, the transplantation of French *opéra-bouffe* to English theatres gave temporary fame. It is not Miss Santley's fault that she was born without the capacity of understanding such a part as Mr Gilbert has written for her. But none the less must we pity the author whose daintiest conception is so inadequately presented.

Here indeed, was proof of the necessity for Gilbert to look outside the realm of *opéra-bouffe* for a cast which would prove sufficiently amenable to accept the new style of performance both in singing and acting. As a start for the casting of *The Sorcerer* three singers were engaged—Alice May, from Australia, for the soprano lead; Giulia Warwick, a mezzo-soprano with only "Grand Opera" experience in the Carl Rosa Opera Company; and George Bentham, a tenor from Her Majesty's Opera Company—more "Grand Opera"! Then came two actresses, one very experienced, Mrs. Howard Paul for the part of Lady Sangazure, and Miss Harriet Everard to play Mrs Partlet. Then Gilbert did, however, go to *opéra-bouffe* for a well-known actor, Richard Temple, for the part of Sir Marmaduke, thus leaving only two more roles to fill. These were the two most important, John Wellington Wells and the Rev Dr Daly, both of whom had to be, first and foremost, really good actors and, in the case of Dr Daly, a good singer as well. Here Gilbert and Sullivan were faced with a real problem. Fortunately for them Mrs Howard Paul was able to help. She made it a sine qua non of accepting the part of Lady Sangazure, that a young actor whom she felt had great potentialities should be given a chance; this despite the fact that he was far from being an experienced actor. So Rutland Barrington was engaged to play the part of Dr Daly!

During this time Sullivan had seen a young professional entertainer at the piano who, whilst disclaiming any pretence to being a singer, said that he could manage the patter song "My name is John Wellington Wells." This was good enough for Sullivan, who had already spent many weeks in holding auditions, and off he sent him to Gilbert. As it happened, Gilbert had already met this young man some months previously and rehearsed him as the Judge in an amateur production of *Trial by Jury*, and on the strength of this they offered him the lead in the new opera. Grossmith hesitated to accept for, as he said, "Look at the risks I am running. If I fail I don't believe the Young Men's Christian Association will ever engage me again because I have appeared on the stage, and my reputation as a comic singer to religious communities will be lost for ever." But Mrs Howard Paul successfully persuaded him to take the risk!

Now to anyone who knows *The Sorcerer*, for a director to cast a complete novice to the stage, in the part of John Wellington Wells, implies either supreme confidence on the part of the director in his ability to train actors or the lunacy of despair! But this is what happened and we must turn to the Press notices to see how this gamble paid off—for there is no gainsaying that it was a gamble to offer the role upon which the opera pivots, and a tremendous acting role it is too, to someone who had never truly trod the boards before, for the part of the Judge which Grossmith had portrayed as an amateur, is played sitting on the bench the whole of the operetta.

In fact looking at things with a cold, impersonal eye, the cast chosen for an operetta which required from all the performers a high standard of acting combined with an equal standard of singing, did not look too hopeful. Three singers— two from "Grand Opera", in which, in those days, acting was non-existent, a third a newcomer to the country and an unknown quantity as an actress; two experienced actresses; one experienced actor, and one with very limited experience; one "entertainer at the piano", and a chorus of students from the Royal Academy of Music.

Finally, to make matters a little more difficult, it was a production which would require a style of performance new to even the experienced members of the cast.

And now to the Press notices—

Regarding the "singers", we find:
Alice May

> ". . . an attractive and graceful Aline." *The Daily News.*
> ". . . a trifle exuberant in style." *The Hornet.*
> ". . . she earned her first laurels on the vast continent of Australia; and, apparently, she has not yet learned to modify the scale of her accomplishments to this very limited land." *Figaro.*

Giulia Warwick

> ". . . sang delightfully and would, had she shown the possession of any dramatic talent, have been successful." *The Hornet.*

George Bentham

> ". . . had a sore throat" [O Tempora! O Mores!]

And now we turn to the actresses:
Mrs Howard Paul

> ". . . excellent from the dramatic point of view." *The Daily Telegraph.*
> ". . . voice not all that it was . . . she looked and acted the part most charmingly." *Figaro.*

Harriet Everard

> ". . . as good as usual." *The Hornet.*
> ". . . too much praise cannot be awarded . . . for her demure Pew-Opener; like Mr Grossmith, she enters thoroughly into the eccentric seriousness of the Author's grotesque idea." *Punch.*

The actors:
Richard Temple

> ". . . both dramatically and vocally good." *The Observer.*
> ". . . promises to be a most valuable addition to the scanty list of singers who can act as well as sing." *Figaro.*

Rutland Barrington

> ". . . made a successful debut." *The Daily Telegraph.*
> ". . . won the chief honours of the evening, by his unforced, self controlled and quietly humorous acting." *Hornet.*
> ". . . by his good taste and freedom from exaggeration he preserved the character of the Vicar from any suspicion of impropriety . . . he will certainly make his mark on the stage." *Figaro.*

The "entertainer at the piano":
George Grossmith

> ". . . displayed remarkable histrionic abilities." *The Daily Telegraph.*
> ". . . remarkable talents as an actor . . . he is at once the least self conscious and most humorous of all entertainers." *Figaro.*
> ". . . The Sorcerest Sorcerer that I ever did see." *Punch.*

The students:
Chorus

> ". . . excellent." *The Times.*

The critic of the *Daily Telegraph* took a broader view of the potentialities of the cast as a whole when he wrote: "There may not have been anywhere on the stage talent of the highest order, but there was a degree of all-round merit which will, in a little while, do complete justice to the opera".

These notices can be regarded as a triumph for both Gilbert and Sullivan and their sponsor, Richard D'Oyly Carte. As far as can be gleaned from remarks by the latter, they had had only three to four weeks intensive rehearsals before the opening night. Gilbert and Sullivan were fortunate in working with Richard D'Oyly Carte, who gave them a free hand in the preparations for the Savoy Operas and, irrespective of cost, allowed them all the time they demanded for rehearsal.

The Sorcerer had also a great significance in the development of the Gilbert and Sullivan Operas for, as Ashley Thorndike wrote:

> The Sorcerer helped him [Gilbert] find the actors and singers for whom he must make appropriate parts and find the general pattern into which he must work. His invention was now quite ready for the stupendous task of filling these requirements with originality and variety.[1]

This was true, for the casts of all the Gilbert and Sullivan works which followed were based upon this pattern; soprano, mezzo-soprano, contralto, tenor, light baritone (the Grossmith parts), baritone and bass. But although Gilbert had the pattern he had yet to find the perfect cast and, certain as he was of his own capabilities, he realized that his success as a director could only be "so far as the limitations of our actors would allow for it" (interview with Bram Stoker).

And now having assessed the capabilities of the performers by the Press notices let us be so bold as to put two and two together and see how the director and his methods stand up to the same assessment. First the "singers".

Although one critic used the words "attractive and graceful" it was obvious that even Gilbert failed to curb the excessive exuberances of the soprano, Alice May, who was sadly out of character with the part of the gentle Aline. Giulia Warwick was another "singer" who was unable to respond to the Director. Of the tenor the least said the better. It is not surprising to find that none of these singers was re-engaged, in fact Alice May did not last the run of the work.

Next come the stage-trained performers. They received acclaim but one can surmise that excellent as Mrs Howard Paul's performance was, it was Harriet Everard who truly responded to the Director's aims. Of the two "actors" it was

[1] op. cit. p. 547.

	1877 Sorcerer	1878 Pinafore	1880 Pirates	1881 Patience	1882 Iolanthe	1884 Ida	1885 Mikado	1887 Ruddigore	1888 Yeomen	1890 Gondoliers
SOP.	May and another	Howson and five other sops. including B. Roosevelt	Hood and three others	Braham	Braham	Braham	Braham	Braham	Ulmar	Ulmar
MEZ.-SOP.	Warwick	Bond	Gwynne (U.K.) (Bond in U.S.A.) Aug. U.K.	Bond	Bond	Bond	Bond	Bond	Bond	Bond
ALTO.	Howard Paul and Everard	Everard	*Cross (U.K.) Barnett (U.S.A.) Aug. U.K.	Barnett	Barnett	Brandram	Brandram	Brandram	Brandram	Brandram
TEN.	Bentham	Power	Power	Lely	Lely	Lely	Lely	Lely	Pounds	Pounds
BAR.	Barrington	Barrington	Barrington	Barrington	Barrington	Barrington	Barrington	Barrington	Denny	Barrington
BASS	Temple	Temple	Temple	Temple	Temple	Temple	Temple	Temple	Temple	Denny ·
L. BAR.	Grossmith	Grossmith	Grossmith	Grossmith	Grossmith	Grossmith	Grossmith	Grossmith	Grossmith	Wyatt

* Everard was cast but illness prevented her appearing. She died in 1882.

In the last two productions, Utopia and The Grand Duke, the only two of the old school to appear were Brandram and Barrington. Brandram joined the Company at the time of The Pirates.

not surprising that the man of experience, Richard Temple, under Gilbert's direction gave a very good performance. But what of the less experienced Rutland Barrington? Admittedly Mrs Paul had said that "he is a young man with great potentialities", but to take this actor and in the space of three weeks encourage, or teach him, if the term is preferred, to give a performance which drew such notices from the Press was tribute indeed to the Director. And finally, to quench any doubt that in *The Sorcerer* was to be seen the work of a first-class director, there was the case of Grossmith, another young man with great talent who, again in the same three weeks of rehearsals, was able to make a triumphant debut in the lead of a new production. The performances of these two were indeed a triumph for Gilbert and his methods and the three men, Temple, Barrington and Grossmith appeared together in all the Savoy Operas for the next ten years. Harriet Everard would have continued also but, after the next production, she had to retire from ill-health and she died in 1882.

Gilbert's work as a director fell into two categories, each complementary to the other. First there were his initial essays into this, for him, new field of stage direction. It is not too far-fetched to suggest that when directing experienced performers he did little more than control the mechanics of the production and make sure the actors gave a true presentation of the characters as he had envisaged them. He had watched Robertson at work, and he now also watched, and doubtless learned much from the well-known performers in his own productions. When in 1874 the Kendals wrote him about *Sweethearts*, asking for his advice, he had already had some seven years' experience as author and director and it is not surprising that he was then able to insist on things going as he wanted them. Ellaline Terriss wrote,

> He was a great stage manager and could show you what he meant, by acting a scene for you. Sometimes having to impersonate a girl's part, being six foot in height and big in proportion, he seemed funny, but he wasn't really, for he con-

veyed even to the ladies the exact way his dialogue should be spoken.[1]

But when Gilbert came to direct the Savoy Operas he moved into the second stage of his work—that of directing and training singers, many of whom were without any stage experience. Now he no longer "*conveyed* the way in which dialogue should be spoken", he *showed* how it should be done —a much more positive action.

Decima Moore, who played Casilda, gives this description of being taught how to speak dialogue.

> He would read a line out clapping his hands between the words to emphasise their rhythm thus: "I've no patience (clap) with the presumption (clap) of persons (clap) in his plebeian (clap) position (clap)!"

Grossmith also refers to Gilbert standing on the stage beside an actor or actress, "and repeating the words with appropriate gestures over and over again, until they are delivered as he desires them to be!" Such methods would be looked upon today with raised eyebrows, but at the time when all this took place, there were no drama schools and Stanislavsky and the "Method" had still to come!

Nevertheless it is interesting to look in on a rehearsal in which Dion Boucicault is directing Marie Tempest. This was at the turn of the century and the play, Somerset Maugham's first play and he, Maugham, tells us,

> his [Dion Boucicault's] method was to work over the first act with the utmost thoroughness. . . . She [Marie Tempest] listened to what Boucicault told her with attention and did it without question. This was not how I had expected a great actress to behave. Of course, she did not slavishly copy him; instinctively, with her wonderful sense of comedy and her mastery of technique, she translated his words into her own language. She took his suggestions, and at once, without any effort that

[1] *Ellaline Terriss*, by herself and with others, Cassell & Co., 1928, p. 86.

47

you could see, gave them originality, colour and life. Her vivid personality transferred them into something definitely her own. It warmed the author's heart to see what she made of his lines.[1]

So the conclusion must be reached that at this stage of his new life as a director, Gilbert was successful with the experienced and talented, but not so with the novice. What would happen in the future? To paraphrase Gilbert's own words "Time alone would tell".

[1] From a programme in the British Theatre Museum.

4

PINAFORE and PIRATES

With two successes to their credit, *Trial by Jury* and *The Sorcerer*, and within five weeks of the opening night of the latter, Gilbert started planning the next G. & S. opera. This would be a real test. Could he and Sullivan pull it off a third time?

For this work Gilbert turned once more to satire and this time directed his barbs towards "the Establishment" when he sketched out the plot of *H.M.S. Pinafore*. This was a plot concerning social inequality and the intrusion of the civilian into the traditions of the Royal Navy. Sullivan was very taken with the plot and when he was given the libretto became very enthusiastic about his share of the production—the music. So far so good, for both the partners were sure of their own capabilities and skill as author and composer.

But whilst Gilbert, the author, was at work, Gilbert, the director, was looking over his shoulder and as the writing progressed so also the characters became clearly defined, their inter-relationship noted and the setting in which the story would take place firmly envisaged. With this setting, the quarter-deck of "H.M.S. Pinafore", the perfectionist was seen at work for, when the curtain went up five months later, there was an exact replica of the quarter-deck of a man-of-war. Not one detail was incorrect thanks to Gilbert's visits to Portsmouth and his watchful eye. Furthermore, with the few exceptions that were to point the satire, the behaviour of the officers and crew was in strict accordance with the etiquette of Her Majesty's Royal Navy.

Rutland Barrington who played Captain Corcoran, said, some years later, "One of the secrets, if not the all-important one, of the phenomenal success of these operas lies in the serious manner in which the delineation of each and every part should be sustained." It was this reality which brought the characters to life and, by avoiding any suggestion of artificiality, pointed the satire. I myself recall an occasion a few years ago when a famous Sea Lord came to a performance of this work at the Savoy and remarked upon the portrayal of the Captain. "I could have sworn that the actor was ex-R.N.," he said, "and he was a perfect Captain Corcoran." As a matter of fact the actor in question had only played the part a few times but he had served in the Royal Marines during the war and had drawn upon real life on board ship for his bearing and behaviour in the opera. Gilbert also insisted that all the uniforms had to be made by the naval tailors in Portsmouth and not entrusted to a theatrical costumier.

As to the casting of the work, Gilbert had four proven performers as a start; Grossmith, Temple, Barrington and Harriet Everard leaving him to find a new soprano, mezzo-soprano, and a tenor. For the soprano part of Josephine he engaged a newcomer, Miss Emma Howson, and for the mezzo-soprano or soubrette role, another novice to the stage, Miss Jessie Bond, while George Power was given the tenor role of Ralph. Gilbert had not re-engaged Mrs Howard Paul, experienced actress as she was, for the role of Buttercup, for, to quote Reginald Allen, "Gilbert intentionally wrote her out of the script, and he employed this indirect means of causing a waning and probably domineering star to leave the company of her own accord".[1]

And how did the newcomers fare on the opening night? Emma Howson received rave notices from most papers including *The Times*—

Miss Emma Howson, who made her first appearance in this country, is one of the brightest, liveliest little ladies imaginable.

[1] Reginald Allen, *The First Night Gilbert and Sullivan*, Heritage Press, New York, 1958

She has a voice of charming quality, pure, sweet and admirably in tune. Her singing at once establishes her in the good graces of the audience and her acting was full of intelligence and comic talent. Her debut was a complete success.

Of course there had to be one critic who thought differently, (there always is) and in *Figaro* this was found, "Josephine is a silly and colourless character, and its exponent has a curiously unsympathetic and harsh speaking voice". Nothing about her singing or performance and in any case this critic was so scathing about the whole performance, when all others were enthusiastic, that his opinion can be ignored. I have been unable to find any comment by either Gilbert or Sullivan upon Miss Howson's performance and it *may* be significant that she did not complete the run of this production. In fact, according to records compiled by Witts-Rollins, no fewer than five other artists appeared as Josephine during the run, among them Blanche Roosevelt who later made such a success as Mabel when *The Pirates of Penzance* was first produced in New York. On the other hand Miss Howson played the title role in *Patience*, in 1882, in America, so she did apparently come up to Gilbert's standard. In any case, as we who have worked in the theatre know only too well, principals, especially on the distaff side, come and go for reasons other than those of their abilities as performers!

George Power, the tenor, received good notices on all counts, singing, acting, and appearance (this must have been a great relief to the authors) and Jessie Bond was given a kindly mention for an "agreeable" performance. It is in the case of Miss Bond that we can see Gilbert, the director-teacher at work. Rutland Barrington many years later said of Miss Bond when he first met her at rehearsals of *H.M.S. Pinafore*, "She struck me at rehearsal as being a rather stodgy, not over-intelligent type of girl, showing few signs of the strong personality and great artistic capabilities that were to make her a firm favourite with the public in a short time." It is obvious that Gilbert was able to see, if Barrington were correct, that under a not specially enchanting exterior were great acting possibilities and what's more, he had complete confidence in his own ability to bring these out. In this he was successful, for four years after her first "agreeable" notice she received the following for her performance in the demanding role of Iolanthe—"[she] may be credited with all the grace, delicacy and fascination we should expect from a fairy mother and her singing of the really exquisite melody . . . one of the most successful items in the entire opera". Then came *Princess Ida* when, as Melissa, she was "the distinct hit of the evening". Two years later she played Mad Margaret, one of the most exacting roles in all these operas, which requires a great range of acting ability as well as excellent singing, and "she surprised everyone by the intensity of her acting". She followed this with her outstanding performance as Phoebe in *The Yeoman of the Guard*, and so in ten years this "rather stodgy and not over-intelligent type" became, as far as Gilbert would ever allow such a thing, a "star". She had obviously the Director to thank for this success and, of course, her own hard work and receptivity to his instructions. So after *Pinafore*, one more "permanent" was added to the team.

But one must not evaluate the ability of the director solely on the progress of Jessie Bond, for with each new production his team had to take on completely different and, in many cases, strongly contrasted roles. Grossmith changing from John Wellington Wells to Sir Joseph Porter; Barrington from Dr Daly the Vicar to Captain Corcoran, Temple from Sir Marmaduke Pointdextre to Dick Deadeye and so on. Gilbert, in his direction, demanded from his actors not a superficial resemblance to the character they were portraying, none of the "different costume same person" technique of previous years, but a carefully worked out portrayal of a real person. This, as I have said before, was a new departure in comic opera and it was a basis upon which the style of these works was set and, some ninety years later, this is still true.

With the success of *H.M.S. Pinafore* firmly established it came as a shock when, at the end of the first year, business troubles arose. The agreement between the Comedy Opera Company and Richard D'Oyly Carte was due to end on July 31, 1879, and so D'Oyly Carte decided to carry on on his own. He secured a renewal of the sub-lease of the Opéra Comique from the lessee, the Earl of Dunraven. He then appointed his manager, Michael Gunn, as his substitute with power of attorney, and then left for New York to arrange the American production of *H.M.S. Pinafore*.

This did not suit the Director of the Comedy Opera Company who sacked Gunn and posted a notice saying that D'Oyly Carte was no longer the manager. Gunn refused to accept this ruling and the Directors attempted to obtain a High Court motion to restrain Gunn from retaining possession of the theatre and interfering with their management. The motion heard on July 29 failed.

On July 31, when the company's lease expired, during the 374th performance a gang of ruffians, hired by the Directors, forced their way onto the stage and tried to remove the scenery and props. The curtain was quickly lowered and a battle royal took place. History has it that Little Buttercup did sterling work in helping to repel the intruders. The inevitable lawsuit followed and Richard D'Oyly Carte won the day and *H.M.S. Pinafore* sailed on a calm sea for another three hundred odd performances!

Then came *The Pirates of Penzance* and once more Gilbert showed himself a director of no common order, in fact I doubt that a schedule of productions similar to those of this work has been attempted again. Four companies, all under Gilbert and Sullivan's personal direction, opened in America within the space of seven weeks. New York, December 31, 1879; Philadelphia, February 9, 1880; Newark, New Jersey, February 16, 1880; Buffalo, February 21, 1880. Then back to London on March 3, and the first night on April 3.

For the American première the cast included a number of

importations from the English Touring Company and the notices were excellent for all except the tenor, over whose performance a discreet veil had better be drawn. Had it not been for the illness of Harriet Everard there would have been only one newcomer in a leading role in the London production of *The Pirates*, the soprano Marion Hood who played Mabel. All the others were cast straight from *Pinafore*; but through sudden illness another outsider, Emily Cross, was called in at two days' notice to play Ruth, and she held the fort with great distinction until the return of Miss Barnett from the American production.

On examining the notices of this production there can be found signs of a more discerning appreciation of the G. & S. Operas and the performances themselves. *The Times*—which had felt that in *H.M.S. Pinafore* the libretto was not truly worthy of Sullivan's gifts (the critic said of the musician, "His true field of action is after all genuine emotion . . .", and then went on to praise Sullivan for his supreme gift of emphasizing "comic points to indicate hidden irony with a slight touch of exaggeration.")—with more understanding, said of *The Pirates*,

> Music is fully able to deal with broadly comic phrases of human life, but Mr Gilbert's characters are not comic in themselves, but only in reference to other characters chiefly of the operatic type, whose exaggerated attitude and parlance they mimic.

This was quite true and if there were any doubt as to the validity of this there is Gilbert's own subtitle, "A New and original *Melo-dramatic Opera*". It was in fact a burlesque on nineteenth-century Italian opera with a musical score which, although parodying this style, offered light music of the highest order. But, even more important to the audience, although they may not have realized it, was the admirable style with which this rich comedy was presented. No cheap comedy playing under Gilbert's direction but true pointed

OPERA COMIQUE.

Licensed by the Lord Chamberlain to Mr. BARKER, 299, Strand.

Lessee and Manager - - - - Mr. D'OYLY CARTE

On SATURDAY, APRIL 23rd,

And Every Evening, an entirely New and Original Æsthetic Opera, in Two Acts, entitled

PATIENCE;

OR,

BUNTHORNE'S BRIDE.

Written by W. S. GILBERT.

Composed by ARTHUR SULLIVAN.

PRICES OF ADMISSION :—Orchestra Stalls, 10s.; Balcony Stalls 5s. and 4s.; (Front Row, 6s.); Private Boxes, £1 1s. to £3 3s.; First Circle, 2s. 6d.; Amphitheatre, 1s. 6d.; Gallery, 1s.

Refreshment Department under the Management of Mr. H. DODSWORTH.

Box Office open daily from 11 to 5. No Booking Fees.

Programme of 1881.

On SATURDAY, APRIL 23rd, and Every Evening,

An entirely New and Original Æsthetic Opera, in Two Acts, entitled

PATIENCE;

OR, BUNTHORNE'S BRIDE.

Written by W. S. GILBERT.   *Composed by ARTHUR SULLIVAN.*

Reginald Bunthorne	...	(a Fleshly Poet)	Mr. GEORGE GROSSMITH
Archibald Grosvenor		(an Idyllic Poet)	Mr. RUTLAND BARRINGTON
Mr. Bunthorne's Solicitor	...	... ...	Mr G. BOWLEY
Colonel Calverley...	... ...	...	Mr. RICHARD TEMPLE
Major Murgatroyd	...	Officers of Dragoon Guards	Mr. FRANK THORNTON
Lieut. the Duke of Dunstable...			Mr. DURWARD LELY

CHORUS OF OFFICERS OF DRAGOON GUARDS.

The Lady Angela	...		... Miss JESSIE BOND
The Lady Saphir	...	Rapturous Maidens	Miss JULIA GWYNNE
The Lady Ella	...		... Miss FORTESCUE
The Lady Jane	...		Miss ALICE BARNETT

AND

Patience ... · ... (a Village Milkmaid)   Miss LEONORA BRAHAM
(Her First Appearance at this Theatre.)

CHORUS OF RAPTUROUS MAIDENS.

ACT I.
EXTERIOR OF CASTLE BUNTHORNE.

ACT II.
A GLADE.

The Opera produced under the personal direction of the Author and Composer.

The Scenery by JOHN O'CONNOR. The Æsthetic Dresses designed by the Author, and executed by Miss FISHER. Other Dresses by Mr. NATHAN, Messrs. G. HOBSON & Co., and Madame AUGUSTE.

NOTE.—The Management considers it advisable to state that the Libretto of this Opera was completed in November last.

On SATURDAY, April 23rd, there will be NO FIRST PIECE. The doors will be opened at 8.0, and the Opera commence at 8.30. On subsequent nights the doors will be opened at 7.30, and at 8.0 will be played

IN THE SULKS.

Vaudeville by FRANK DESPREZ and ALFRED CELLIER.

Mr. Liverby...	... Mr. W. H. SEYMOUR
Joseph...	... Mr. FRANK THORNTON
Mrs. Liverby	... Miss JULIA GWYNNE

Followed by "PATIENCE" at 8.45.

OPERA GLASSES on Hire of the Attendants, 1s. 6d.—may be retained all the Evening,

Coffee and Ices of the Attendants.

The MUSIC will be published in a few days. Orders taken by the attendants will be executed post free on the day of publication.

comedy as can be seen from the notices. "Grossmith's make-up and demeanour as the Major-General were excellent; the mixture of dry, quaint humour and caricatures of military sternness have been happily combined." No touch of burlesque here. Of Frederic, a part which can be "just another juvenile lead" and a dull one at that if played incorrectly, "Mr Power acts Frederic just in that simple-minded way that brings out most strongly the absurdity of the character". Temple "was a capital representative of the Pirate Chief of old-fashioned melo-drama and gave his music with amusing exaggeration". Marion Hood did well, although according to *The Times*, "Further careful study may make an excellent singer of Miss Hood."

It was in the next production, *Patience*, that the team was completed when a new soprano and tenor were found who stayed the course for seven years. George Power, in spite of his very good notices, left at the end of the run of *The Pirates*, and was replaced by Durward Lely, and Leonora Braham became the new soprano. There was one more alteration in the contralto roles when Barnett left for personal reasons in 1884 and she was replaced by her understudy, Brandram, who continued up to the end of the G. & S. partnership. This stabilizing of the cast certainly made life easier for both Gilbert and Sullivan who now knew the capabilities of their principals and could write accordingly. But most important of all to Gilbert was the knowledge that his cast of performers were able to sink their own personalities and take on those of the characters in the play. And so the G. & S. Operas continued to delight the British audiences for the next decade.

Performers are only human and it is natural, in particular when playing comedy, that during a long run they get "ideas", and unless this creative urge is checked the whole performance can be thrown out of perspective and—especially in the case of satire—the style can be completely ruined. This is where Gilbert the disciplinarian stepped in. No variations or additions of business were permitted. The eye of the Direc-

Abstract of Week commencing 29 th Dec. 1 .... 1879, **and ending** 3rd Jan 1 18 70

Theatre.	Bill.	Day.	Weather	Gross Receipts.	REMARKS.
Sthle. N.Y.	First week. Pirates of Penzance	M.		Theatre	Abond for rehearsal of New Piece
		Tu.		Theatre	closed for rehearsal of New Piece
		W.	Slush	3948.25	First Night of Piece.
		Th. 1	Fair	1405.75	Only under first New Years Day.
		F. 2	Snow	1467.75	
		S. 3	r. fine	1570.25	
		Mat 3	rain	910.50	Only under first – New Years Day.
		Mat 3	v. fine	1321.50	
		Total ...		**8024.00**	

CURRENT EXPENSES.

Salaries	1320.00
Share of Preliminaries	837.40¾
Sundries	519.75
Current Travelling Expenses	102.89
Total Current Expenses ...	**2780.04¾**

Gross Receipts .... 8024 + 34.30½ Sax½

Current Expenses ... 2780.04¾/?

Lesse's Share .... 3199.60 } 5984.64¾

Profit 2073.65½ Loss 2073.65½P

Shares £91. 21 ½.

Record of week in New York.

tor was perpetually on the London productions and the touring companies were under the watchful eye of the Stage Manager who either dealt with any such misdemeanours himself or, if necessary, referred them to the London Office. From Gilbert's own letters comes the following which speaks for itself. In 1889 he wrote to Mr James, who was playing the comedy roles in one of the touring companies.

> . . . The principle of subordination must be maintained in a theatre as in a regiment. I find on enquiry that Mr Carte's grievance does not refer to your altering the dialogue but to the introduction of *inappropriate, exaggerated and unauthorised business* . . . no actor will ever find his way into our London Company who defies authority in this respect.[1]

Even Rutland Barrington who, as one can imagine, after thirteen years in the company was looked upon as a valued member called down upon his head Gilbert's wrath for gagging in *The Gondoliers*. Gilbert wrote to Mr Carte registering a complaint on this score ending, *"it must be played exactly as I wrote it"*.

It was not only on the acting side that discipline was imposed for François Cellier who was Musical Director for over thirty-five years, when not engaged in London, travelled Great Britain holding rehearsals and conducting the touring companies. Thus was the standard maintained and this discipline certainly proved its worth.

Gilbert has been called autocratic, not without due cause it must be admitted, but he could not have been completely inflexible in his direction. He said himself that no matter how clear was the conception in his own mind as to how a part should be played, he was inevitably limited by the performers own capabilities, excellent as they were. The opinion is also held that too strict a discipline when imposed upon actors can be frustrating but surely this is only necessary when the actors themselves are not self disciplined. I am reminded of a

[1] Letter in Gilbert's Papers (British Museum Collection).

performance by two of our greatest comedians of the 1930's who played a scene together in a musical comedy which ran for over two years. One of the performers, the late Leslie Henson, told me many years later, that throughout the whole run the timing of that scene, some five to six minutes, never varied by more than a couple of seconds. He and his partner had worked out the business of this scene of broad comedy to the last detail and never varied it at any performance. But not all actors control their performances and without the discipline, or autocracy, that Gilbert exercised there is little doubt that the style in which these works should be played would have become obscured.

DELINEATION OF CHARACTER

No matter how skilful the direction of the mechanics in a production, if the delineation of characters is not clear cut, the performance will lack conviction. This is especially true when a series of works is presented each with the same team of performers. With writers of less stature than Gilbert and Sullivan, this could easily have become the case and, popular as the artists were, the public would have come merely to see Mr Grossmith or Mr Barrington playing some role or other in their own inimitable way, instead of coming to see Mr Grossmith as Ko-Ko or Jack Point, or Mr Barrington as the Captain or Pooh-Bah. It was primarily the *stage* characters that drew them to the theatre. As a result, although principals have come and gone, the operas have survived.

There is no need to comment upon the marked contrasts between the roles played by Barrington, Temple, Bond and Barnet, for they are obvious to all, but in the roles for the soprano and tenor, which could be ranked as "juvenile" parts, the contrasts are there too but they are more subtle. Consider Ralph in H.M.S. *Pinafore* and Frederic in *The Pirates of Penzance*. Here are two characters who, in musical comedies, would be the "young heroes", and who would be handsome, sing well (we hope), make love to the heroine and marry her in the end. In other words, just stock characters. But not in Gilbert and Sullivan. Apart from their youthfulness they have nothing in common. Ralph has been brought up as a humble sailor and is a simple uneducated lad—in spite of his incredible vocabulary—but he is prepared to defy authority and social rank in order to get his girl, the Captain's daughter. On the other hand Frederic, who has been brought up with a bunch of pirates, is the slave of duty who will always "act in accordance with the dictates of his heart, and chance the consequences". He is, in fact, a prig of the first water, albeit of considerable charm.

The two young ladies in these operas are also of very different character. Josephine, the Captain's daughter, is a spoilt beauty and a snob who tells the humble sailor to "cast your eyes upon some village maiden in your own poor rank— they should be lowered before your Captain's daughter". At the same time she is torn between her love for this sailor and her duty to her father. "I have a heart and therefore I love; but I am your daughter, and therefore I am proud." Mabel, the Major-General's daughter, is a real soldier's daughter with all the militant outlook upon life that is expected of such a one. A girl whose idea of encouraging the police force is this:

> Go, ye heroes, go to glory!
> Though you die in combat gory,
> Ye shall live in song and story—
> Go to immortality!

A girl of tremendous character who, although deeply in love, will face up to life according to her upbringing. . . . "No, I'll be brave! O family descent! How great thy charm! Thy sway how excellent!" The satire here is directed to the beliefs of "The Colonel's Lady".

In all these roles throughout these operas there can be found such indisputable indications of character.

If ever Gilbert wrote any parts in these operas that could have become vehicles for "star" performances, they were the light comedy roles; John Wellington Wells, Sir Joseph Porter, Ko-Ko and so on. But thanks to his strict control over his actors, control which has been maintained by the D'Oyly Cartes ever since, these impersonations have remained faithful to his intentions. In demeanour these characters were true to life, although their actions may sometimes have been at

64

Iolanthe, a Sadler's Wells production.

Ruddigore, cartoon film designed by T. Pettengall and J. Cooper;
directed by Joy Batchelor.

"A Sorcerer young man
A Pinafore young man
A Brilliant what I call quite
Ille-yacht-ical
Balladry Bab young man."
Gilbert on his boat *Chloris*.

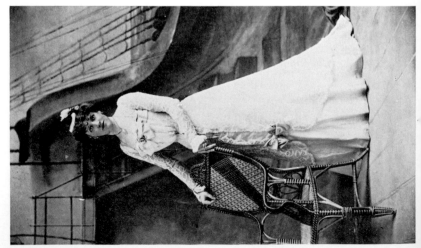

Ruth Vincent
as Josephine,
1899.

variance with reality. The Lord Chancellor, for example, apart from his youthful mistake of marrying a pretty young girl who was, in fact, a fairy, behaves throughout as one would expect the head of the Judiciary to act—strictly in accordance with the Law. Ko-Ko is a little tailor suddenly promoted to high office and, in spite of the deference shown by all with whom he comes into contact, he still remains his humble, bewildered, self.

Let us finally look to the contralto roles. Here is a group of characters about which there has been considerable misconception. Much criticism has been levelled at Gilbert for his gibes against the middle-aged, frustrated spinster, for—so it is sometimes said—he portrayed them cruelly in his operas. But such a generalization does not stand up to an objective examination: a more acceptable suggestion, I feel, is that Gilbert did not dislike the middle-aged woman, except when she tried to appear and behave younger than her years.

The first of Gilbert's middle-aged women, Lady Sangazure and Mrs Partlet in *The Sorcerer*, were both widows with grown daughters and they both find second husbands. So much for frustration! Then came Mrs Cripps, better known as Buttercup, in *H.M.S. Pinafore*; a rumbustious widow carrying on the business of bum-boat woman, who was on the best of terms with the sailors, who also gets a second husband— Corcoran.

It was not until *The Pirates of Penzance* was written that any justification of this criticism is found. Here, for the first time, is presented a middle-aged spinster, Ruth, who is in love and wants to marry Frederic, a lad of 21, whose nanny she had been. There are two other characters which it could be said are drawn with an uncharitable pen, Katisha and Lady Jane. The bloodthirstiness of the former can be accepted as being in keeping with what may be presumed to be the Japanese way of life at that period; but she does want to marry a man very much younger than herself, and, when she finds this is no longer possible, settles, in a despair of loneliness, for

Ko-Ko, "this miserable creature". Lady Jane's non-stop pursuit of Bunthorne throughout the opera is pure comedy; but this is marred, unfortunately, by her blatant self-pity in her solo, "Silvered is the raven hair". However, Gilbert the Director gave her some outrageously comic business with a cello, in the recitative which introduces this song, which helps to soften the cruelty of the lyric.

Of the remaining middle-aged women, one, the Duchess is married and the others, with the exception of Lady Blanche, all get partners of suitable age and station.

It is interesting to find documentary evidence of the fact that even Sullivan, on one occasion at least, misunderstood Gilbert's intention with regard to the portrayal of one of these women, as the following letters show:

Sullivan to Gilbert, July 1, 1893.

The part of Lady Sophy [*Utopia, Ltd.*], as it is to be treated in the 2nd Act, is in my opinion a blot on an otherwise brilliant picture, and to me personally, unsympathetic and distasteful. If there is to be an old or middle aged woman at all in the piece, is it necessary that she should be very old, ugly, raddled, and perhaps grotesque, and still more is it necessary that she should be seething with love and passion (requited or un-requited) and other feelings not usually associated with old age. I thought that 'Katisha' was to be the last example of that type—(a type which however cleverly drawn can never be popular with the public, as experience has taught me)—because the same point was raised then, and you even modified a good many of the lines at my request. . . . A dignified, stately, well made-up and well dressed elderly lady is a charming feature in a piece, and can be of real service to the composer, because the music he writes for her is so well contrasted with the youthful bustle of the other elements. On the other hand, the elderly spinster, unattractive and grotesque, either bemoaning her faded charms, or calling attention to what is still left of them, and unable to conceal her passionate longing for love, is a character which appeals to me vainly, and I cannot do anything with it. Let me here *most emphatically* disclaim any idea of calling your

66

judgment to account—that is not my intention—artistically and from your own point of view you may be right.

I am only giving you my own personal feeling in the matter —telling you what I like and what I don't like. I like every word you have given me hitherto of the new piece, and I don't like the prospect of Lady Sophy in the 2nd Act. Furthermore, I am sure you won't take offence at my plain & outspoken opinion, for I court [an] equally frank opinion from you on anything in my share of the work which you don't like or which doesn't fit in with your intention.

Yours ever sincerely,
A. S.

Gilbert to Sullivan, July 3, 1893.

Dear S

As you know, I am always most anxious to meet your views in every respect and I believe I have never laid myself open to the charge of raising captious objections and making unnecessary difficulties. But the fault you now find with Act 2 brings me absolutely to a standstill. When I read the very elaborate sketch plot to you at Roquebrune last January—or early February— you expressed full and unqualified approbation of every incident in the piece. Not to take advantage of a hasty or ill-considered expression of approval on your part, I left with you a verbatim copy of my sketch plot that you might digest it at your leisure. Since then I have worked steadily at the piece (save during the ten weeks of my illness) and at least five-sixths of it are finished. A fortnight or so ago (nearly five months after I read the plot to you) I received for the first time an intimation that you disapproved of the Lady Sophy business in Act 2 and made a suggestion the exact purport of which I did not gather from your letter, and so, while falling in at once with all your other wishes, I left the Lady Sophy business to be discussed when we met. It now appears, as I gather from your letter of today, that you wish her to be in Act 2 a grave and dignified lady to be taken seriously and apart from any grotesque suggestion. But (to say nothing of the fact that by investing her with a pathetic interest I should be laying myself open to the charge of repeating Mr Grundy's treatment of the

Brandram part in the last act of *Haddon Hall*) I have in Act I committed her irrevocably to a more or less humorous fate, and in this you have aided and abetted me. Surely to make a sudden *volte-face* and treat her in Act 2 as a serious or pathetic personage (there being no single serious note in the piece up to this point) would be to absolutely stultify myself in the face of the audience. Possibly I may even now have failed to grasp your intention in its completeness. Possibly you may have failed to grasp mine. Most assuredly it is not necessary that she should be 'very old, ugly, raddled or grotesque'—she may be and *should be* (as I explained to you on Friday) a dignified lady of 45 or thereabouts, and no more ugly than God Almighty has made the lady who is to play the part. Nor do I propose that she should be seething with love and passion. She is in love with the King (as a lady of 45 may very well be with a man of 50) —but her frenzy is not that of the gross or animal type at all, as you seem to imagine. Her position is this. Being compelled, by her duties as governess to the young princesses, to impose upon herself a restraint and an appearance of prudishness which is foreign to her nature, she takes the opportunity of being alone to express her natural dislike of conventional shackles. This she does in a strong quasi-dramatic scene (or by some other form of musical expression) with enough of suggested humour in it to keep it in harmony with the humorous and satirical character of the piece—and in this she declares her impatience of the Quakerish restraint which her position as the governess of the Princesses imposes upon her and her regret that, having regard to the scandalous conduct which is attributed to the King in the *Palace Peeper*, she cannot accept attentions which, but for these considerations, she would gladly do. The King overhears this with infinite pleasure and explains that the pars were all written by him. Embarrassed at the turn affairs have taken she is nevertheless bound to admit, now that his character is cleared, that the King is not wholly indifferent to her. She and the King, having thus come to an understanding, indulge in a joyous duet leading to a dance, which is witnessed and joined in by the two princesses and their lovers.

Now I am no apologist for my own humour. It is very likely that all this may be poor fun indeed, but in a matter of good taste I claim to be as good a judge as any man alive, and I cannot for the life of me see that in what I propose to do with Lady Sophy the canons of propriety are in the smallest respect disregarded. One thing is quite clear to me—this difficulty can be best settled by a personal meeting. If you think so too I will run down to you on Thursday next—or, if that won't do, on Tuesday the 11th—and I have no doubt we shall come to a pleasant understanding on this very important point.

Yours very truly,
W. S. Gilbert

And out of all this came a quite innocuous impersonation of a dignified middle-aged gentlewoman whose behaviour conformed to that expected from one of her class and breeding.

In the remark, "no more ugly than God Almighty has made the lady who is to play the part" (which does seem rather unkind), Gilbert did not intend to imply that the actress Miss Brandram was plain, for in an interview in The New York Tribune, in 1885, about The Mikado, he had referred to her "as a personable young lady who has no objection to 'make-up' old or ugly . . . and of her goodnatured readiness to sacrifice her own personal attractions to the exigencies of the part, we have, perhaps, taken an undue advantage."

An interesting observation was made by the French writer Augustin Filon, who said of Gilbert,

Gilbert had felt the need more than once of providing some sort of musical accompaniment for his paradoxical fantasies, for is not music the natural background to the land of dreams? This accompaniment seemed to soften the outlines of his thought and to temper the bitterness of his satire.[1]

Maybe these two letters show that influence at work?

[1] Augustin Filon, The English Stage, John Milne, 1897, p. 152.

6

GILBERT AND HIS DIRECTION OF THE CHORUS

Any suggestion of sterile formalism or stereotyped traditionalism in a G. & S. production was avoided by Gilbert when he evolved one of his revolutionary canons of stage direction; that of bringing the chorus to life, making them an integral part of the stage picture. Isaac Goldberg, the great American authority on G. & S., speaking of *Trial by Jury*, goes as far as to compare them with the Greek chorus when he says, "The chorus forms a logical offspring of the plot and often assumes the function of the Greek chorus, acting as commentators upon the proceeding."[1] Throughout the whole of the G. & S. Operas the chorus was assigned to play a vital part and never were they used merely to dress the stage. If their reactions to the drama, and therefore to the actions of the principal characters, were done mechanically, they would have shed a cloud upon the scene instead of high-lighting it, and upon the direction of the chorus Gilbert lavished as much detailed care as he did upon the direction of his principal actors. Ninety years later I heard another master in the art of writing and directing comedy, Noel Coward, say "there can be no real acting without complete co-operation of colleagues; especially in comedy."

The first step Gilbert took towards the carrying out of this rule, was to insist that each member of the chorus was a real character and not just a "singer in costume". This was a revelation to performers as well as audiences. Critics found

[1] Isaac Goldberg, *Sir Wm. S. Gilbert*, Stratford Publishing Co., Boston, U.S.A., 1913, p. 89.

Savoy Theatre
2nd Jan / 1882

To
W. S. Gilbert Esqr.
Arthur Sullivan Esqre.
R D'Oyly Carte Esqre.

Gentlemen,

We the Gentlemen of the Chorus beg to thank you very sincerely for the very thoughtful and handsome present you have made us, it is appreciated very much by all not only on account of its value but as showing that our exertions have met with your approval. It comes as a pleasant surprise because nothing like it has been experienced in any Theatre before, in fact it is even a greater novelty than the Electric Light.

We feel sure that it will not be forgotten but will act as an additional inducement to us all to do anything in our power to further the interests of the management.

Hoping that the New Year prove as successful as the last and wishing you health and happiness in the "coming bye and bye."

We remain, Gentlemen.

Yours faithfully,

Geo. J. Parris
Charles Ramsay.
E. Hall Davenport.
C. Kelly Lyster.
Geo J. Hamilly
P. Ashford
Evelyn Vernon
C. J. Muntetti
Henry Searle

Chas Sander
Hetting Morgan
W. Denhaue
F. Ainsworth
J K Pearce
C Noude.
Lucy Burbank
Harris Tresoro.
S. Allen
L B. Clifford
H. Hurst

Testimonial.

themselves watching for the first time a completely integrated body of people at work in a light musical entertainment.

As the curtain rises in *Trial by Jury* the interested and eager jurymen and spectators offer an animated scene. Indeed throughout the whole opera, although they are seated in groups on each side of the stage and have to react en masse to the action, they can still find ample opportunity for controlled self-expression. Here is no formal "point to the right, point to the left, all nod heads" method of production, but one in which an intelligent response is asked of every performer.

Although, according to Gilbert's own prompt book, the original setting of the chorus in the opening of *Trial by Jury* was static

```
x  x  x  x  x  x  x  x  x  x  x  x
o  o  o  o  o  o  o  o  o  o  o  o
```

this was changed to a more realistic one with the chorus strolling about in pairs as they sang and taking their places in their respective boxes when the Usher enters. In *The Sorcerer* the opening chorus was also static and here we find the first of the geometrical groupings that were used frequently throughout the operas. But in *H.M.S. Pinafore* there is a complete breakaway from this type of grouping. Sullivan had written an extended introduction to Act I and this was done obviously at the request or with the approval of the author, who used this period to set the scene. When the D'Oyly Carte Opera Company produced *H.M.S. Pinafore* in New York in November, 1879 an American critic wrote,

> It seemed already as though human ingenuity had been exhausted to provide appropriate business for the opera and that everything thinkable had been thought of. But last night's performance was everywhere studded with new points. When the scene opened the sailors were all seen at work, flemishing [*sic*] down the ropes and attending to various ship's duties while the whole was under the supervision of the busy and important Midshipmate.

72

This gave an animation to the first scene that it generally lacks. Practicable shrouds were set, with sailors clambering up and down and the chorus was skilfully divided, some on the gun deck, and some on the quarter-deck, so as to destroy the usual unpleasant stiffness in grouping.

The "lack of animation and stiffness of grouping" mentioned in this passage referred to the pirated American productions.

Once the opera got under way, Gilbert did group his performers in formal patterns. On specific occasions, such as the entry of the Captain and the First Lord of the Admiralty, this grouping was in accordance with naval procedure, but when the Officers and Sir Joseph retired, the sailors assumed a more relaxed grouping and were clearly off duty. When the whole company was on the stage Gilbert used his "semi-circle and straight-line" method of dressing the stage.

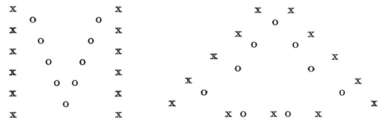

Today such grouping is regarded as out-of-date and it does tend to root performers to one spot for long periods, broken only by some slight movement, but it had one great virtue; it did leave plenty of space on a small stage, such as were those in the theatres in which the operas were originally played, to provide an adequate acting area for the principals and it also helped underline the vital focus of attention in the grand ensembles. I myself was interested a few months ago to see an example of exact geometrical grouping of the chorus at Glyndebourne Opera House in a performance of *The Magic Flute*, and it was very appropriate to the scene and completely acceptable to my modern eye.

It is important to bear in mind that Gilbert used these geometrical groupings as the basis only of his direction of the chorus. They were not, as is sometimes thought, an end unto themselves. Here are some typical groupings in *Patience*. In each case the chorus is so placed that it forms a background to the principals; a background which can change in design by means of simple movements.

PATIENCE. Finale Act I.

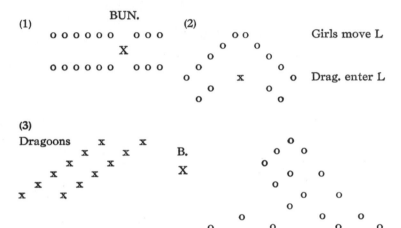

But never, even if there were no change in groupings, was it allowed to remain static. It was indeed the mirror which reflected each passing image of the drama and it was given detailed reactions at salient points.

Here is a page, once more taken from an original prompt book of Gilbert's, which shows how important he regarded this side of stage direction.

Song and Chorus—Sir Despard. *Ruddigore*, Act I.
"Oh, why am I moody and sad?"

Girls: "Can't guess!"	Girls shake heads.
„ "Confess!"	„ hands up.
„ "Oh yes"	„ nod to each other.
„ "Ah why?"	„ forward.

„	"Fie, fie!"	„	finger up.
„	"Oh, my!"	„	arms up.
During symphony		„	speaking to each other.
Girls: "Like you."		„	pointing.
„	"It do."	„	to one another.
„	"How true!"	„	arms up.
Sir Despard: "I once was a nice-looking youth;"		„	all look.
Girls: "A trice"		„	explaining to each other.
„	"That's vice."	„	„ „
„	"Not nice."	„	disgust.
Sir D: "Indeed I am telling the truth!"		„	speaking to one another.
Girls: "That's we."		„	to each other.
„	"Like me."	„	indicating themselves.
„	"May be."	„	eyes down.
Sir Despard: "You are very nice looking indeed!"		„	bob.
Girls: "Just so."		„	nod.
„	"No! No!"	„	arms out.

In the opening scene of *Ruddigore* between Dame Hannah and the Bridesmaids are to be found the following directions as to the reactions of the Bridesmaids to the situation:

Zorah: We shall be disendowed—that will be the end of it! Dame Hannah—you're a nice old person—you could marry if you liked. *(All assent)* There's old Adam *(movement)*— Robin's faithful servant—he loves you with all the frenzy of a boy of fourteen. *(All assent)*

Hannah: Nay—that may never be, for I am pledged!

All: To whom?

Hannah: To an eternal maidenhood! *(Turn to one another)* ... one of the bad Baronets of Ruddigore *(movement)*. . . . My child, he was accursed! *(movement—all interested)*

During Dame Hannah's song with which this scene ends the Bridesmaids remain still until the following stanzas.

Each lord of Ruddigore *(All lean forward)*
Despite his best endeavour

75

Shall do one crime, or more,
Once, every day, for ever! *(Movement)*
This doom he can't defy
However he may try,
For should he stay
His hand, that day
In torture he shall die! *(Ladies cover faces with hands)*
The prophecy came true
— — — — — — —

In agony he died! *(All forward—ladies "oh!" hands to face)*
Chorus: And thus, with sinning cloyed, etc. *(To one another)*

The above examples are but two of many to be found in G. & S. and it does not require any great amount of thought to see how far Gilbert had progressed from the work of his predecessors in the field of musical entertainment.

It was evident that Gilbert was acutely aware of one of the great attributes of a good actor—the ability to *listen* intently and was always insistent that, when the occasion arose, the chorus did so and reacted accordingly. In *Iolanthe* there are some outstanding examples in the author's original prompt book. In the Lord Chancellor's opening speech which commences, "By all means, etc." the instructions to the assembled Peers are as follows:

at "... think proper to select"	all bow.
"... render her exceptionally happy"	all 'hear, hear' *very quietly.*
"... marriage with his own ward?"	all shake heads dubiously.
"... without his own consent?"	ditto
"... contempt of his own court?"	ditto
"... arrest of his own judgment?"	all shake heads but more forcibly.
"... such thorns as these!"	all sigh sympathetically.

Later when Lord Tolloller sings "Spurn not the nobly born" the instructions are:

Chorus exhibit in action the sentiments expressed by the singer—during the ballad Peers sit and stand grouped in attitudes of despair—at the end Peers stand with arms extended in imploring attitudes.

Again on page 12 of the libretto of *Iolanthe* the following is found:

All: "Given!"
Phyl: "Yes, given!"
All: "Oh, horror !!!" *(Hands above heads and backs turned.)*
Recit.—Lord Chancellor *(to Mountararat).*
"And who has dared to brave our high displeasure,
And thus defy our definite command?"
(Peers in action ask same question.)
Enter Strephon.
Strephon: " 'Tis I—young Strephon! mine this priceless treasure! Against the world I claim my darling's hand!"
(All threaten Strephon.)

Note the direction of the Peers—"Peers in action ask same question", for in this detail we see at work a director who was not satisfied to have a chorus merely looking on, but who insisted upon intelligent and personal participation in the action.

Once more in the finale of Act I when the fairies sing "Let us stay madam etc". Gilbert wrote and underlined "*All this requires animated gestures on the part of the chorus*". It is interesting to note that in both this instance and the earlier one when he says "Chorus exhibit in action etc." there is no documentary evidence to show that he had evolved a formal plan of gesture to be used at these moments. He wanted individual, natural reactions and not mechanical arm waving or finger wagging.

A "musical" without dancing is unheard of and in this respect the G. & S. operas followed the convention of the day. Gilbert was not a dancer himself so he called in an expert to help him with this side of the production; John D'Auban, who

77

Iolanthe

~~PEROLA.~~

DESCRIPTION OF STAGE BUSINESS.

𝔓𝔯𝔦𝔫𝔱𝔢𝔡 𝔓𝔯𝔦𝔳𝔞𝔱𝔢𝔩𝔶.

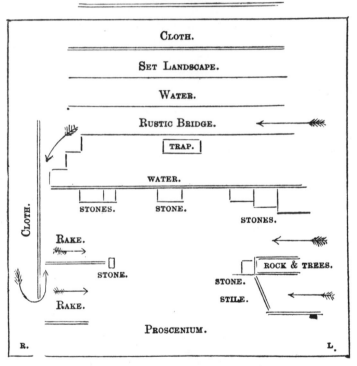

Rough Stage-plan, Act I.

arranged the dances for all the operas except *Thespis* and *The Gondoliers*. Here stereotyped work is found, the same meaningless dance steps in the introduction of a song, regardless of the content of the lyric. For instance what relationship does the following routine in the orchestral introduction to Hildebrand's song, "Now hearken to my strict command on every hand", in Act I of *Princess Ida* bear to the lyric? "Gents take Ladies R hand, raise them up, 2 bars, Lower hands, 2 bars. Repeat with other hand and turn." A somewhat similar inspiration incorporating a "court step", when used for the introduction to the finale of *Iolanthe*, is not inappropriate as an expression of light-heartedness, but any more profound feeling than a mild gaiety cannot be found anywhere when dance steps are used in these operas. There is one notable exception, *Utopia Ltd.*, which will be discussed later in this chapter.

The reason for the simplicity of D'Auban's dance steps was undoubtedly the fact that he was dealing with singers who had not learnt to dance, but a more enlightened outlook would have been welcome.

In all other aspects of the bearing of the individual chorister, Gilbert was meticulous in his direction. He would not tolerate an approximation or theatrical compromise unless the latter was absolutely unavoidable, as he felt when he made a note regarding the Peers in *Iolanthe*—"Peers being dressed in white silk tights do not *actually* kneel but seem to do so".

The most outstanding example of this meticulous care for detail was when *The Mikado* was produced. The following acknowledgement was given in the programme.

The management desires to acknowledge the valuable
assistance afforded by
Directors and native inhabitants
of the
JAPANESE VILLAGE, KNIGHTSBRIDGE.

Thanks to the help given by these visitors to the Great Exhibition, the performers were carefully coached in deportment, the use of the fan, and make-up. D'Auban worked with a Japanese dancer in arranging the dances. One of the most interesting movements made by a principal in this work is to be seen in the steps made by the Mikado as he moves across the stage singing "My object all sublime". These steps are adapted from one of the Kabuki dances of the God of Vengeance and, when done correctly, are terrifying in their threat of retribution.

It was Agnes de Mille who, in 1943, discarded conventional choreography in the theatre when she arranged the dances for *Oklahoma* and dancing then became a significant part of a "musical" and not mere visual titillation. But Gilbert with his foresight, fifty years before in 1893, had suddenly realized that dancing was a medium for expression of specific moods and in *Utopia Ltd.*, for the first time ever, instructions are given as to the mood of the dance.

At the end of the duet between the King and Lady Sophy comes a "Dance of Repudiation" by Lady Sophy. Following the chorus "Eagle High" there is music for a grand ceremonial dance. An even more important example in this new use of dancing is found in the trio for the King, Scaphio and Phantis, where the King has to dance and so express, first "complete indifference" and secondly "unruffled cheerfulness" while the other two express (also in dance) "remorselessness". Finally in the opera, there comes the "Graceful Dance" for the King and Lady Sophy "dancing affectionately together" followed by a wild Tarantella in which they are joined by others.

It was also when producing this opera that Gilbert went to endless trouble in his demand for authenticity in the presentation scene at the court of the King in Act II. In order that this should be exactly as it was at Buckingham Palace, the assistance of a well-known society lady was enrolled who saw that everything was done according to the etiquette of Queen Victoria's court. In the possession of Miss D'Oyly Carte there

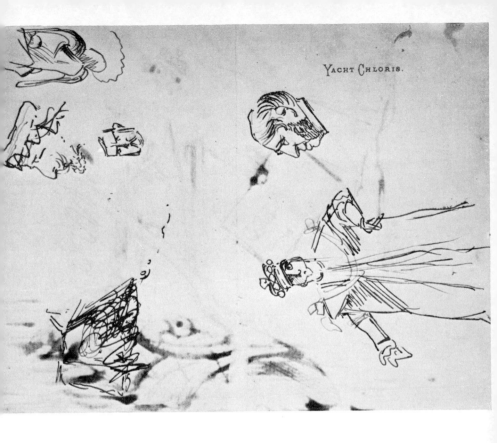

YACHT CHLORIS.

Above: Sketch of a Yeoman of the Guard by Gilbert.

Right: Miscellaneous sketches by Gilbert.

Gilbert at home.

A Peer of Gilbert's Realm.

is a drawing of one of the presentations at court which was used as a guide in arranging this scene.

In the theatre of today a good chorus is the accepted thing and as much care is taken in engaging and directing them as is the case with the principals. A production in which this essential element has been neglected is unheard of. But to Gilbert must go the credit for being the first of the great writers and directors of English operetta to think in this way and thanks to his direction "the cultivation and intelligence of the choristers" (George Bernard Shaw) enabled them to play their full part in the success that these operas have enjoyed for so long a period.

7

THE GILBERT TRADITION

The word "tradition" has been used constantly in reference to the productions of the G. & S. operas by the D'Oyly Carte Opera Company and in some cases this has implied adverse criticism. Before continuing let us ask "what is tradition?" The following definition appears to be the most reasonable— "A custom so long continued that it has almost the force of law;" far more reasonable than Gustav Mahler's—"Tradition is laziness", and Toscanini's—"Tradition is the last bad performance".

Miss Ann M. Lingg wrote in an American magazine (*Opera News*, January, 1962) an article "The Bogy of Tradition" in which she asked "What is tradition?" Without waiting for an answer she continued in somewhat confused prose:

> A word open to so many interpretations that it has become the most abused term in the performing arts. How one feels about it is a matter of personality, education, experience and even metabolism, part of his general picture as a human being; whatever he says about it expresses his basic attitude towards the old and the new, evolution vs revolution. Depending on where he digs his heels on the long path between the Victorian and the avant-garde, he is either for tradition or against it, and vociferously so.
>
> The problem was spot-lighted twelve years ago when the D'Oyly Carte Company toured this country with its productions of Gilbert and Sullivan. Every detail of the original performances, many decades old, was being maintained at a time when the "feud against tradition" had become a catch

phrase in the long-haired world. . . . The Tyrone Guthrie productions and our own American Savoyards have proved that the G. & S. Operas need not be frozen in time to keep their appeal!

With regard to the last remark I would reply, first of all "That is a matter of opinion!", and second that the final words should have read ". . . have proved that the *productions* of the G. & S. Operas etc", for it is surely the productions and not the operas themselves that are under discussion.

The first target for the arrows of the "anti's" is the mechanics of the presentation, and, at first glance it may appear that criticism on this ground is justified, for there can be little if any merit in slavishly retaining such instructions as "X enters U S R", or "the chorus stand in a semi-circle", despite the fact that this is according to the original production. What *is* important is that the impact of X's entrance is retained or that the grouping of the chorus is related to the purpose of the scene.

It is not unreasonable to draw attention to the fact that the presentation of these works is an integral part of the works themselves for as Gilbert wrote so did he visualize the production as a whole. Evidence to support this conjecture is to be found in the rough drafts of some of his plays and this ability to visualize scenes in action as he wrote them was surely one of the great attributes of Gilbert and his production was as much an integral part of the G. & S. operas as were the "words and music".

So when discussing the pros and cons of the merit of maintaining, over the years, the original production it is Gilbert's own conception we are looking at and not the superimposition of the ideas of a second-rate contemporary stage-manager upon work of genius.

It was never necessary for him to hand over his libretti to a stage director to remould into a working script. He knew, not only what he wanted, but how to realize his intentions

Thro' ensemble Bum × to L then up stage C, Ladies following him on knees with outstretched arms, he then comes down & finally sits on seat L C with Ella's head on his knees – Zafhir R of him, Ang C of Stage. Col × to Ang, followed by major – Jane comes down from steps & stands at back of seat R C. Duke R.

Jane

Louise Maj.   Col. Ang   Zafh. Bum Ella

0 major stage back to R corner – Col further C. + Duke × to Jane

Patience. Gilbert's note facing:

> Though my book I seem to scan
> In a rapt ecstatic way,
> Like a literary man
> Who despises female clay,
> I hear plainly all they say,
> Twenty love-sick maidens they!

on the stage. It is true that he accepted certain of the contemporary conventions of the day but he developed them along his own lines. The following reproduction of a page from the prompt book of a production of *Cymbeline* at the Sadler's Wells in 1859 could have come from one of Gilbert's own prompt books of any of the G. & S. operas, but it was his genius for bringing alive and maintaining the sense of reality that lifted his productions out of the run of mere mechanics.

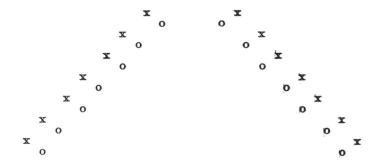

But even in what may appear to modern eyes to be a relic of Victorianism, signifying lack of invention on the part of the director, there may be far more than meets the eye. Take for instance, the counter-marching which occurs as the chorus sing the Allegro Marziale with which the finale of Act I of *Iolanthe* ends. In the first section in E flat, the fairies and the Peers march briskly up and down the stage as they threaten each other. Then, when with the modulation into A flat, the mood changes to one of sarcasm, they all remain still; the change of mood being reflected by a similar change in the action. With the return to the original mood and a repetition of the music of the first section, the marching is resumed, reflecting in simple terms, the conflict of the two groups.

Marching and counter-marching is not, as is sometimes supposed, just a relic of nineteenth-century burlesque and pantomime, but was an accepted vehicle as a means of expression in a stage spectacle. The outstanding productions of opera in Europe at this time were those of Bayreuth and George Bernard Shaw writing in 1894 of a performance of *Lohengrin* reports:

> After the combat with Telramund . . . the men, greatly excited and enthusiastic over the victory of the strange knight, range themselves in a sort of wheel formation, of which Lohengrin is the centre, and march round him as they take up the finale in the principle key. When the modulation comes, the women, in their white robes, break into this triumphal circle, displace

the men, and march round Elsa in the same way, the striking change of key being thus accompanied by a correspondingly striking change on the stage. . . . Here you have a piece of stage management of the true Wagnerian kind, combining into one stroke a dramatic effect, a scenic effect, and a musical effect, the total result being a popular effect the value of which was proved by the roar of excitement which burst forth as the curtains closed in.[1]

This is precisely what Gilbert had devised, on a very much smaller scale, twelve years earlier in 1882. Shaw says that a more complex example of the same combination was afforded by the last act of *Tannhäuser*, which produced the same outburst from the audience. He adds. . . .

> I have over and over again pointed out the way in which the heroic expenditure of Sir Augustus Harris [Director of Covent Garden] gets wasted for want of a stage manager who not only studies the stage picture as it is studied, for instance, at the Savoy Theatre . . . but who studies the score as well and orders the stage so that the spectator's eye, ear and dramatic sense shall be appealed to simultaneously.[2]

So it follows that any new version of a scene such as the one in *Iolanthe*, must offer three elements, dramatic, scenic, and musical, and the presentation of these must be done in such a way as to be true to the intentions of both author and composer.

Now "*traditional*" delineation of the G. & S. characters is a very different matter and something that cannot be dismissed with a supercilious raising of the eyebrows, for the characters which were born of Gilbert the author's mind, were presented in live terms by Gilbert the director, and there could be no possibility of disagreement between these two! He said on one occasion "the impression conveyed to the audience was almost invariably a reflex of my conception and intention". Keeping to the traditional mechanics of a production can be

[1] *Shaw on Music*, Doubleday & Co., New York, 1955. p. 124.
[2] ibid.

regarded as senseless, but to retain the author's conception of the character cannot be looked upon as bowing to tradition, but just plain commonsense. To alter drastically the author's image of a leading character will inevitably result in throwing the whole plot out of balance and leave the audience bewildered, especially in a musical play in which the music mirrors clearly both the character as well as the action. Should the basic conception of the character be changed it will become at variance with the music and the result will jar.

There must be evolution if progress is to be maintained, but evolution is something which is based upon what has gone before and not the result of complete repudiation of the past. It is seventy years since Wilde's *The Importance of Being Ernest* was first produced, and during that time there have been many notable productions of this sparkling comedy. The decor, costumes and mechanics of each production have been different but still, whether it be Dame Edith Evans or Miss Pamela Brown playing Lady Bracknell, the fundamental character remains constant, and no cry of "tradition" is heard! How many Eliza Doolittles have appeared on the stage, in film or in *My Fair Lady* and all of them have been a simple cockney flower-seller. Is this obeying the author's conception or would the "long-hairs" call it "just tradition"? What differences there have been in these performances are not due to any deliberate alteration of the original impersonation, but are the result of the performer's own personality and skill adding, albeit unconsciously, an individual quality to the playing of the part.

The cry of "tradition" is occasionally raised with regard to the speed at which certain well-known songs in G. & S. are sung; in particular the so-called patter songs. Before a logical conclusion can be arrived at as to whether this criticism is justified, it is necessary to consider first how Sullivan related the music to the character. First he ensured that when the character changed from speech to song he did so without any alteration in his natural speed of delivery. "As a man speaks—

87

so shall he sing", was one of the golden rules of Sullivan's collaboration with Gilbert; thus consistency of characterization was maintained throughout. A typical example of this is found in *The Gondoliers* when Don Alhambra goes from speech into song when telling the Ducal party of the fate of the young Prince. He prefaces his song with a speech ending, "In the entire annals of our history there is absolutely no circumstance so entirely free from all manner of doubt of any kind whatever! Listen and I'll tell you all about it." Then, with exactly the same dignified delivery, he continues the narrative in song. Sullivan marked this song *Allegretto non troppo vivo* and this is, as near as can be indicated in musical terms, the tempo of the Don's normal speech. Thus the transition from speech into song does not alter the impersonation. The rare occasions when the natural speed of delivery is altered, is when the mood of the person changes and this is reflected in the music.

Then there are settings which have additional qualities. An excellent example of this is the trio in *The Mikado*, Act I, when Pooh Bah, Ko-Ko and Pish-Tush discuss the situation which has arisen by reason of the Mikado's impending visit to Titipu. First, the pompous Pooh Bah delivers his opening remarks in his usual portentous manner to an equally portentous melody.

Then Ko-Ko gives the reason for his reaction to the situation in musical terms which admirably reflect the anxiety with which he propounds his specious arguments, as he attempts to justify his unworthy behaviour.

Pish-Tush then comments dispassionately upon Ko-Ko's worries and does so to a matter-of-fact melody, the musical equivalent of his own aloof attitude to the whole affair. In each case the music reflects the character and the mood whilst, at the same time, enabling the performer to maintain the correct speed of delivery. Sullivan has marked this trio *Allegro non troppo vivace* ♩ = 84.

There is, however, one song in particular where Sullivan's

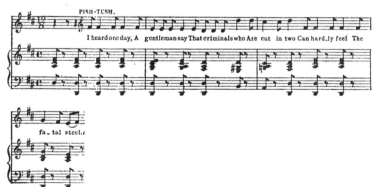

indication of speed is ignored in the traditional performance. This is the song with which the Lord Chancellor introduces himself in *Iolanthe*, "The Law is the true embodiment".

In the vocal score this is marked *Allegro vivace*, but it is always sung *Allegro non troppo* and this has given rise to considerable argument when a conductor has tried to insist upon the printed instruction being obeyed. That this alteration is not the result of an arbitrary action upon the part of a performer in the past will be shown by an examination of the facts.

In the full score the tempo given is *Allegro vivace* but it is wise to remember that Sullivan wrote very quickly (for example he "re-composed", as he put it, the Overture to *Iolanthe* between midnight and 7.0 a.m. on November 21, 1882) and there is little evidence in the ms of the full score of any alterations other than the corrections of a few wrong notes. If any modifications were necessary they were made at rehearsals. That these were not included in the vocal scores, in the case of *Iolanthe* in particular, can be put down to the fact that these were being prepared by the printers long before rehearsals began, for these scores were published four weeks after the London première.

All this could be considered conjecture but there is, in my

opinion, incontrovertible proof that the speed at which this song is sung in the D'Oyly Carte performances is the one agreed upon by both Gilbert and Sullivan. In order to prove this is correct let us turn and examine the impersonation of the Lord Chancellor in these productions and find out upon what grounds this can be taken as an authentic portrayal of Gilbert's intention.

The facts are these—Grossmith, the first Lord Chancellor, was directed by Gilbert and it can be taken for granted that the speed at which he sang this song was in accordance with the wishes of both Gilbert and Sullivan. His successor, Henry Lytton, rejoined the company in 1887 and remained in it until his retirement from the stage in 1934. During this period he worked under Gilbert, playing many roles and so it is reasonable to assume that when he took over the comedy roles in 1909 in the Principal Repertory Company, he was presenting them as the author intended. In fact, as Gilbert's letters show, anyone who did not play a part as he laid down it should be played was never promoted to the London Company. As is recorded on p. 61 above, a comedy actor named James, who was a well-known member of one of the touring companies, came under Gilbert's extreme displeasure on account of a persistent insubordination. Or that is how Gilbert saw it. The much more famous Rutland Barrington—who one might have thought to have been above criticism—was also in Gilbert's bad books for some time because of his gestures of independence in interpretation. "It must be played *exactly as I wrote it*": that was the alpha and the omega of the Gilbertian creed.

So we come back to Henry Lytton who personified the authority of tradition throughout his long career. Lytton, of course, was closely associated with that other traditionalist François Cellier. Cellier was musical director of the D'Oyly Carte company for more than 35 years and when he was not engaged in London was travelling throughout Britain—and further afield—conducting performances and also holding rehearsals. We can, I think, have no doubt as to the authenticity of Lytton's performances backed by Cellier's knowledge and skills.

Then came Martyn Green, who as Lytton's understudy based his work upon that of the principal, but whose own personality gradually made itself felt when he took over the roles on Lytton's retirement. With reference to the song in question, Martyn Green told me that he took it at the same speed as did his predecessor; furthermore it should be looked upon as a "point" and not a patter song. Added to this is the fact that my friend and one-time colleague Isidore Godfrey, whose authority cannot be questioned, confirmed this matter of tempo when I discussed the matter with him when I joined the company. And so through the performances of Peter Pratt to the present Lord Chancellor, John Reed, the speed has remained, to all intents and purposes, constant. So, with regard to the printed indication, all this points to one of two conclusions: either Sullivan's *Allegro vivace* was a slip of the pen or, when he came to rehearse the number, he altered the tempo to suit the character. Hence the "traditional" speed. This also goes to show that it is unwise to condemn any performance on the grounds of "tradition" without due consideration of the facts of the case.

Miss Lingg, in her article quoted earlier in this chapter, gives an interesting example, which has a bearing upon this acceptance as sacrosanct of a printed instruction.

> Helping to coach the cast for *The Rake's Progress* at the Metropolitan a few years ago, associate conductor Ignace Strasfogel carefully followed the original metronome marks; but when Stravinsky came to rehearsal he demanded faster tempi. Which is the more authentic, the printed score or word of mouth transmission by those present?

So-called "tradition" in G. & S. performances is not just blind obedience to custom, but the following of an unbroken continuity of direction which has existed from the first performances to the present. This is unique in the annals of the English Theatre.

8

THE NEW PRODUCTIONS

"It is absolutely essential to the success of this piece that it should be played with perfect seriousness throughout."

"An eccentric actor need not let the audience know that he is eccentric!"

"Grimaces are derogatory to the comic actor's art."

"There must be no exaggeration in costume, make-up or demeanour."

"Characters should believe in the perfect sincerity of their words and actions."

"All must be natural and the actors get their effects by doing and saying absurd things in a matter-of-fact way without obvious burlesque of the characters they are presenting."

W. S. Gilbert, 1870/90.

"The foundation of playing comedy is to be truthful to what the author intended and to refrain from guying the comedy. The role must be played straight and the laughter left to the audience."

Athene Seyler, 1964.

"The basis of comedy is in ordinary people being found in funny situations and involved in awkward dilemmas."

Ben Travers, 1964.

On January 1, 1961, English audiences in general, and the D'Oyly Carte Opera Company in particular, were going to be shown just how G. & S. should be produced; for on that date, the copyright would expire and productions of these operas would be open to all. In swift succession came *Iolanthe* and *The Mikado* by Sadler's Wells, *H.M.S. Pinafore* and *The*

93

Pirates of Penzance by Tyrone Guthrie and a showing on BBC TV of a production of *The Gondoliers* from Stratford, Ontario. *The Mikado* ran at the Wells for some fifty or more performances and *H.M.S. Pinafore* and *The Pirates of Penzance* enjoyed a brief season of thirteen weeks between them in London. *Iolanthe* has remained in the repertoire of Sadler's Wells and is seen a few times each season. *The Gondoliers* has, mercifully, stayed in Canada. Any idea that the managements may have had of repeating even in any comparable degree the original successes—*The Mikado*, 672 performances; *H.M.S. Pinafore*, 700; *The Pirates of Penzance*, 363; *Iolanthe*, 398; and to full houses—was quickly dispelled.

It was inevitable that these "free" productions would be compared with the "traditional" ones and, according to the onlooker's point of view, were either acclaimed or condemned. Unfortunately most of the criticism, no matter whether for or against, was almost wholly subjective, and can be classified as "the Old versus the New". What was overlooked, if ever it had been realized—which I doubt—was the fact that the subject under discussion was in reality "the Present-Day Producer versus Gilbert (the Producer)".

It was only to be expected, bearing in mind the evolution in stage decor over the past seventy years and the larger stages now available, that the settings, while still remaining faithful to the opera in question, were, with one exception, a welcome change to today's audiences. There was one innovation in the first act of *Iolanthe* at Sadler's Wells, when, instead of the curtain rising on Gilbert's "An Arcadian Landscape", a close-up of a Fairy Dell was seen, ablaze with gigantic flowers in and under which, the fairies were peeping. Before the entry of the mortals a gauze was flown and the Fairy Dell was then transformed into the "Arcadian Landscape". Gilbert had had, very early in his career as a director, a similar idea for one of his fairy plays. Admittedly this idea was expressed with few characters and on a small scale, but, carried out on a larger canvas, it could well have developed into this "modern" setting—a delightful, imaginative thought carried out beautifully.

The Mikado. This setting has been changed many times in the D'Oyly Carte productions, the most revolutionary one being the new decor and costumes designed by the famous painter Charles Ricketts for the 1926 season at the Savoy Theatre. This came as a great surprise, even a shock, to the public at the time, but it was very soon accepted and regarded as a great advance upon the original. Of course it can be said that it is difficult to go wrong when designing for so definite a costume play and, providing the production is to be upon orthodox lines, that is true.

I have also seen an amateur performance, directed by Anthony Besch, of this work done in modern dress (1965) and I cannot say that I thought it an improvement in any way whatsoever. Above all else it lacked colour and gaiety.

In the cases where the director has had quite revolutionary ideas on the production the costumes have been correspondingly startling.

The setting for *H.M.S. Pinafore* was, as to be expected, a replica of the quarter-deck of a man-of-war and followed Gilbert's first idea by having the poop-deck up stage instead of stage right as it has been for many years in the Savoy productions.

The costumes in the two Sadler's Wells productions and those of Tyrone Guthrie were charming and in period. So far so good.

Then there were the broad mechanics of these productions which differed to a considerable degree from those of Gilbert, but in general, were perfectly acceptable, in fact in a few instances were an improvement or, at least, a welcome change, from what had been seen for so long. But these changes, in decor, costumes and mechanics, were to be expected and were not designed to do more than present a new framework for the operas. What was far more important was the presentation of the characters themselves; how would this be tackled by the modern director? Plenty of talk had been heard of "throwing a new light upon Gilbert", "bringing out the *comedy* of the operas", and so on, and so on; and now the time had come for us to see for ourselves.

First let us look at the performances of the Sadler's Wells principals in general, discussing later the impersonation of the light comedy roles of Ko-Ko, the Lord Chancellor, Sir Joseph Porter and the Major-General. The playing of the sentimental scenes between the young lovers was admirable. Outstanding were those between Phyllis and Strephon in *Iolanthe*. Here was a tender and enchanting young couple, obviously truly in love with each other and the direction in impeccable style in the true *commedia dell'arte* tradition, was very refreshing, completely appropriate to the words and music, and, most important, in accordance with Gilbert's own principles of production. The consistent sincerity with which these parts were played in the original cast at Sadler's Wells would, I am sure, have delighted the authors. In such scenes as these, little help is to be found in Gilbert's own prompt books so it is reasonable to assume that he modified his direction to suit the capabilities, or limitations, of the players. It is also significant that good, straightforward and sensitive direction is all that is necessary to bring such scenes to life. These particular scenes, played as they were at Sadler's Wells could have been put, in toto, into the traditional production without causing any disturbance of, or break in style.

The same could be said of the opening of the finale of Act I in which Phyllis and the Peers overhear and misinterpret a conversation between Strephon and his mother, Iolanthe. This was presented with a realism that pointed the drama neatly and convincingly. The director was helped by having a more flexible set at his disposal than that of the D'Oyly Carte Opera Company. But fundamentally the grouping had much in common with Gilbert's.

Sadlers Wells.

    Iol. O
    Str. X

<pre>
                              Peers
              Mnt.   X   x x x x x x x x x
              Phy.   O
              Tol.   X   x x x x x x x x x

changing to

                      x x x x x x x x x

                      x x x x x x x x x

     O X   X O X
</pre>

at Phy. "Oh, shameless one"

Gilbert.

<pre>
                   x x x x x x x x x

                   x x x x x x x x x

     O X   X O X
</pre>

In Act 2 of *Iolanthe* there was one drastic alteration in grouping and movement that gave point to a song in a manner hitherto unknown. A time-worn convention of the Victorian stage was to allow the principal in his or her one great aria, to come down stage centre and just sing. With the advent of the real "stage" director into the musical theatre, this has been discarded once and for all; not without some heart-burning on the part of some singers, one is bound to add! Only a very short time ago I heard of the case of one of the old school of "Grand Opera" singers of international repute who, at a first rehearsal, in a world famous opera house, of one of her great roles, when the director mentioned the word "production" in relation to her big aria, said, "Production! I don't know what you mean. I always come right down stage and sing this aria straight to the front." And that was that!

So it was a relief to see this principle of "down to the foot-lights and hand it out" go by the board when, at the end of her scene with the recalcitrant fairies, the Fairy Queen sings

G   97

"Oh Foolish Fay". In this song the Fairy Queen's focus of attention shifts from the Fairies in the verse, to the audience in the refrain, which is an aside. This change is very difficult to get over to the listener when the soloist is down stage the whole time and the Fairies are standing in two rows behind her, with heads bent. In the Sadler's Wells version the verse was sung directly to the Fairies who had grouped themselves freely around her and so the change of direction in the aside to the audience was made very clear and without difficulty: the Fairies meanwhile showing, in mime, their distress at the Queen's reproof.

It would appear surprising that a director of Gilbert's calibre was satisfied to accept, at this point a time-worn and senseless convention, but, in point of fact he did not. At least not if one is to believe the evidence in his own prompt book. He grouped the players thus:

Fairies

O O O O O O O O O O O O

O O O O O O O O O O O O

O

Fleta

X   O   O   O

Sen.   Cel.   Q.   Lei.

and added these directions:

"Oh amorous dove" (aside)
2nd. verse. "On fire that glows" takes Celia by wrist.

This is different from what has been the grouping for many years:

O O O O O O O O O O O O

O O O O O O O O O O O O

O   O   O

Cel.   Fle.   Lei.

X   O

S.   Q.

Maybe this final grouping was the result of a headstrong Fairy Queen not wanting her "big moment" spoilt by business, and ignoring the fact that she was still addressing the Fairies.

The scene between Phyllis, Lord Mountararat and Lord Tolloller which followed was played with absolute seriousness and so was perfectly in the style of Gilbert's own production and the laughter was left to the audience. But Gilbert would not have approved of the "cod" operatic gestures made by the Sentry as he sang his cadenza in the quartet which ends the scene.

Towards the end of the opera when, as a result of revealing her true identity to the Lord Chancellor, Iolanthe is condemned to death by the Fairy Queen, there is a sudden threat of real tragedy. By accepting the material at its face value and directing accordingly, nothing of dramatic impact was lost. Gilbert's own direction of this scene is completely realistic in conception and it is only the formal grouping of the Fairies in a semi-circle that makes it look a little old-fashioned.

The final picture at Sadler's Wells was a delight, with the Fairy Queen looking ravishing wearing a Guardsman's bearskin, prior to being flown sky high in her floral coach.

This would not have shocked Gilbert one little bit, quite the reverse in fact, for did he not arrange a "Grand Transformation" scene at the end of *Trial by Jury*?

In Tyrone Guthrie's production of *The Pirates of Penzance* three scenes were outstanding. The entrance of the girls in Act I, "Climbing over rocky mountains", was handled in a perfectly natural manner. No longer did they "take up positions" in set groups, but just behaved as would any party of young girls do on reaching a sandy cove where they intend to spend the day. There was even the Victorian Miss, complete with easel and stool, who started the inevitable watercolour. The scenes which followed continued in similar style and the final one "How beautifully blue the sky", when the girls pretend to gossip about the weather whilst in fact, they are eavesdropping on Mabel and Frederic, was particularly enchanting in its entire naturalness.

The other two episodes were the Policemen's chorus and the scene between the Police and Pirates, in both of which the director allowed his invention for comedy full rein but kept to the style suitable to the period and material. Both direction and performance were most refreshing and would I think have pleased Gilbert.

The Sadler's Wells *Mikado* brought forth no startling innovations for it was produced in a straightforward, workmanlike fashion, full use being made of the facilities for handling large groups that are possible on modern sets. The playing in general was on the lines of a Gilbert production with one outstanding performance by Clive Revil as Ko-Ko. This brilliant actor presented a straightforward portrait of a scruffy little tailor bewildered by his sudden rise to a position of importance and power. There was no straining after effects, no cheap playing for laughs, no "inappropriate, exaggerated business", just a true picture of a fine actor's reading of the part. A reading in which every facet of the devious little tailor's character was clearly presented much to the delight of the audience. I saw this performance more than once and I am sure that playing of such integrity although differing in certain details from "the Gilbert tradition", would have met with Gilbert's wholehearted approval. Certain of the scenes in which the whole company were concerned were impressive by virtue of the larger chorus and greater number of extras at the disposal of the director.

It was the direction of the other light-comedy roles and the introduction of so-called "comic business" that threw the performance out of perspective and destroyed all sense of style in these elegant period pieces. When comparing the G. & S. operas with contemporary *opéra bouffe* William Archer wrote,

The wall which divides the stage of the Opera Comique [at that time the home of G. & S.] from that of the Globe, for years divided humour from inanity, wit from horse play, refinement from vulgarity, literature from the lowest form of literary hackwork.[1]

This appreciation was as true in the *direction* of the operas as the writing thereof.

In each of these productions Gilbert's precepts were swept aside in a self-conscious intention to be funny. It was not possible to believe in the legal integrity of a Lord Chancellor entirely lacking in poise and dignity; the First Lord of the Admiralty with his artificial struttings and his lapse from good taste in expressing his feelings towards Josephine with a typical Gallic gesture, and finally a Major-General whose one claim to distinction was, apparently, the ability to sing a song quicker than it had ever been sung before! These characterizations lacked any sense of reality and were just vehicles for low comedy playing which was in direct variance to Gilbert's demands. Therefore his wit and satire were lost.

In *H.M.S. Pinafore* "comic" playing started when the Captain had finished the first verse of his opening song which he sang standing half way down the companion-way. He then allowed himself to be carried, as if he were a tailor's dummy, across the deck by two sailors and placed in position for the next verse. This *jeu d'esprit* was repeated in *The Pirates of Penzance* when the Major-General, on entering, was not allowed to walk down a few steps but had to be carried, again like a tailor's dummy, by two of the pirates.

But it was not only in the playing of the major roles that the desire to be funny at all costs created such havoc. The Fairies' opening chorus in *Iolanthe* was given a clod-hopping, heavy-handed treatment that implied inability on the part of the audience to savour Gilbert's gentle gibe, "Tripping hither, tripping thither, Nobody knows why or whither". The Entrance of the Peers was obscured in such a welter of extraneous business, with shooting sticks and unceasing

[1] William Archer, *English Dramatists of To-day*, Sampson, Low, etc., 1882.

101

movement, that all the dry wit of the lyric and the satirical majesty of the music was lost. During the exit at the end of the scene the behaviour of a drooling Peer would have been utterly distasteful to Gilbert as indeed, it appeared to be to much of the audience.

I read, in 1963, a notice of Mr Shawe-Taylor's in *The Sunday Times*. Apropos of excessive production in an *opéra bouffe* he says, "This is what they call production; and it said as plainly as can be said that the producer had no confidence in the music and none in the singer either". Mr Shawe-Taylor adds that at this point in the opera his neighbour was heard to sigh "Why can't they leave the bloody thing alone?" This is what I thought when, two years previously, I had seen this travesty of the entrance and march of the Peers.

The famous march which ends Act I was turned into a battle royal between the Fairies and the Peers, once more to the detriment of the words and music and hardly consistent with the style of a Gilbertian phantasy.

Throughout *H.M.S. Pinafore* the deliberate lack of any attempt to maintain even a faint resemblance of naval etiquette on the part of the crew blunted the barbs of the author's satire.

In *The Pirates of Penzance* there was another example of an exaggeration in making a verbal point when the pirates, having freed the Major-General's daughters from the threat of matrimony, sing, "Pray observe the magnanimity etc." In case their gentlemanly behaviour was overlooked by the audience, the pirates adopted, for these few lines only, a phony Oxbridge accent, when all that was needed was an intelligent delivery of the lines.

A final example of disrupting the continuity of the scene was when the Major-General sang his barcarolle, "Softly sighing to the river" in the finale of Act II. Instead of being treated seriously it was performed in the glare of a spot-light on an otherwise darkened stage, lighting reminiscent of the old-fashioned music-hall, in a manner in which little consideration was shown to Sullivan's charming music and so the gentle comedy was distorted.

It is to be deplored that much of what Gilbert had successfully discarded when he directed the G. & S. operas reappeared in these new productions. Before disregarding so blatantly the rules laid down by him it would have been wise to remember what his contemporary, John Hollingshead said of him:

> . . . He was somewhat of a martinet in his stage management, but he generally knew what he wanted, was more often right than wrong and was consequently an able director of his own pieces.

Finally it is worth recalling what William Archer wrote in 1895:

> The victory of Gilbertian extravaganzas over *opéra-bouffe* as adapted for the London market, is the victory of literary and musical grace over rampant vulgarity and meretricious jingle.

Verbum sapienti sat est.

CODA

"Gilbert and Sullivan"—this is the most exciting combination in theatre history. Gilbert had no illusions about the significance of his partnership, for on November 19, 1903, he wrote to François Cellier in reply to birthday wishes:

> Many thanks for your good wishes. Personally I'm rather sick of birthdays—I've so many of them. A Gilbert is of no use without a Sullivan—and I cannot find one![1]

One could also say with justification, "A Sullivan is no use without a Gilbert", for what survives of Sullivan's music today? The Overture *Di Ballo*, *The Lost Chord* and some well known hymns! The remainder of his works, rightly or wrongly [some of them, in particular the music for *The Tempest* and the "Irish" Symphony, wrongly], remain on the shelf, a memorial to what was in some respects a dreary artistic era. Even the ephemeral craze for Victoriana a few years ago did not find its way into the concert hall. It is, therefore, all the more remarkable that the "traditional" productions of the Savoy Operas, far from just holding their own in today's theatre, are breaking all records for attendance in Great Britain, and Canada and America. And when one looks back over the last ninety years of enthusiastic audiences, this takes some doing. The cities in which these new records have been made are not small provincial ones, which rarely are visited by first-class performers, but include the great ones —London, New York, San Francisco, Manchester, Toronto and Montreal.

What is the secret of this success—giving the public what

[1] Post-card in Gilbert Collection (B.M.)

4. Feb: 1891

1, QUEEN'S MANSIONS,
VICTORIA STREET. S.W.

Dear Gilbert

Little did I think that
in asking you to come and
encourage me with your
presence on Saturday, I was
reopening an unhappy
Controversy, which I firmly
believed was settled and
forgotten. We look at things
from such different points of

view, that I fear neither will ever be able to convince the other. You assume I am in possession of facts, of which in reality I am absolutely ignorant; and as you decline to receive the verification which I was desirous of obtaining from the person most competent to give it me, I am afraid the matter must rest where it stands.

yrs truly

Arthur Sullivan.

it wants or giving the public what the authors wanted them to have? It may be difficult to separate these two questions for they do, to some extent, impinge upon each other as a formula for success, but I am sure that the scales are weighted in favour of the latter. Gilbert and Sullivan wrote and produced these elegant, witty satires and laid down the rules as to how they were to be played and so achieved a success that surprised even them. The D'Oyly Cartes, Richard, Rupert and Bridget, have, despite many changes in presentation, preserved (some say too rigorously) these performances. But take note that the changes they have made have only been in decor, costume and "mechanics" and have not, in any way, altered the playing of the characters as laid down by Gilbert. So from some comes the cry of derision "Tradition!"

Surely these are masterpieces of light satire with no complex or subtle undertones and it is a mistaken idea to treat them as profound contributions to the theatre which offer to director and actor many different approaches in interpretation.

In spite of so much that was acceptable and enjoyable in the new productions it was distressing to see so many lapses in the direction which resulted in the clock being turned back to the pre-Gilbert and Sullivan days of opéra bouffe with all its attendant inanities.

BIBLIOGRAPHY

(Except where otherwise stated books published in London.)

W. S. Gilbert Collection, British Museum Add. Mss. 49289-49353 (65 volumes).

Reginald Allen, *The First Night Gilbert and Sullivan*, 1958, New York.

William Archer, *English Dramatists of Today*, 1882.

Edith A. Browne, *W. S. Gilbert*, 1907.

F. A. Cellier and C. Bridgeman, *Gilbert, Sullivan, and D'Oyly Carte*, 1914

Sidney Dark and Rowland Grey, *William Schwenk Gilbert, his life and letters*, 1923.

Charles Dickens, *Essays and Sketches*, ed. M. Alderton Pink, 1951.

Augustin Filon, *Le Théâtre anglais*, Paris, 1896, *The English Stage*, 1897.

Richard Findlater, *The Unholy Trade*, 1952.

P. H. Fitzgerald, *Principles of Comedy and Dramatic Effect*, 1870; *The Kembles*, 2 vols., 1871; *The Savoy Operas and the Savoyards*, 1894.

Isaac Goldberg, *Sir. Wm. S. Gilbert*, 1913, Boston, Mass.; *Story of Gilbert and Sullivan*, 1929.

Gervase Lambton, *Gilbertian Characters, and a Discourse on W. S. Gilbert's philosophy in the Savoy Operas*, 1931.

Henry Morley, *The Journal of a London Playgoer from 1851 to 1866*, 1866.

T. E. Pemberton, *Charles Dickens and the Stage*, 1888.

Ernest R. Reynolds, *Early Victorian Drama, 1830-1870*, 1936, Cambridge.

T. W. Robertson, *Society* and *Caste* (ed. T. E. Pemberton), 1915.

Maynard Savin, *Thomas William Robertson: his plays and stage-craft*, 1950, Brown University Studies, Providence, Rhode Island.

G. W. Smalley, *Anglo-American Memories*, 1911.

Ellaline Terriss, by herself and with others, 1928.

Ashley H. Thorndike, *English Comedy*, 1929, New York.

INDEX